BLUEBOTTLE
GOES TO WAR

Peter Sellers &
the RAF Gang Shows

ALLIED PARIS ENTERTAINMENTS
THEATRE ENSA-MARIGNY - PARIS
N.A.A.F.I.
PRESENTS
E.N.S.A. ENTERTAINMENTS FOR ALLIED FORCES

Week commencing MONDAY DECEMBER 24th 1945 including 25th)
Nightly at 8 p.m.

The R.A.F.	THE GANG-SHOW JIVE BOYS
"GANG-SHOW"	JACK and the BEANSTALK
	etc.
★	100 MINUTES OF
A Ralph READER Production	HIGH-SPEED VARIETY
★	*Sunday December 30th 1945 - CELEBRITY CONCERT*

SPECIAL GALA

Wally SPARKS	Harry HERRING	Geneviève CRAUVILIER, violincello
Cliff HENRY	Cyril WRIGHT	Jean DOYEN, pianist
Bill WILKIE	Larry FOUGITT	Henry MERCKEL, violinist
Freddie BENT	Dave LODGE	Accompanist : André COLLARD
George WHITEHEAD	Leo OSBORNE	
Peter SELLERS	Don COLLIN	Next week : "WALK-UP! WALK-UP!" Gay Circus Revue

Admission free to all allied troops in uniform

All silverware in use at the Marigny Theatre supplied by CHRISTOFLE

GENERAL MANAGER E.N.S.A. PARIS : EDWARD STIRLING
E.N.S.A. Liaison : Francois CLERMONT

BLUEBOTTLE
GOES TO WAR

Peter Sellers &
the RAF Gang Shows

PJ BROWNSWORD

UNIFORM

First published by Uniform
an imprint of Unicorn Publishing Group LLP, 2020
5 Newburgh Street
London W1F 7RG
www.unicornpublishing.org

Every effort has been made to trace copyright holders
and to obtain their permission for the use of copyright
material. The publisher apologises for any errors or
omissions contained within and would be grateful if
notified of any corrections that should be incorporated
in future reprints or editions of this book.

Cover photographs: Peter Sellers/The Lynne Unger
Children's Trust, IWM & author's collection.

10 9 8 7 6 5 4 3 2 1

ISBN 978-1-913491-01-7

Designed by Matthew Wilson
Printed by Gomer Press

CONTENTS

INTRODUCTION

In the archives of the Imperial War Museum in London are kept two reels of 35mm film catalogued as 'RAF Gang Show, Akyab Island, Burma'. The footage, of excellent quality, shows a group of men in khaki air force uniforms, arriving at their latest stopover, unloading baskets of gear and then taking to the stage that has been improvised for them – a haphazard construction of war-damaged timber and corrugated iron. Among them is a rather skinny young man, with a confident air, taking the lead in some staged hi-jinks for the camera, and later, playing the drums as part of a jazz quintet and acting in a two-handed sketch. His face is instantly recognisable now, though at the time the film was made, he was just nineteen years old and quite unknown. He is Aircraftman (2nd Class) 2223033 Richard Henry Sellers, and the world remembers him as Peter Sellers*.

Sellers served in the Royal Air Force for over three years; however, this period of his life has been largely overlooked in the wealth of material written about his later career. Now, for the first time, the story can be told, with the help of RAF records in the National Archive, as well as newly discovered films, photographs and contemporary reports.

*he was always called Peter, from a young age; this had been the name of his elder brother, who died in infancy.

Sellers in India, wearing a forage cap.

The Sellers family, who came from the world of variety and vaudeville, had left London on the outbreak of war in 1939, moving to Ilfracombe in Devon. This also coincided with the end of Peter's formal education: the legal age for school-leaving at the time was fourteen. He spent the next four years doing odd jobs in local theatres, learning to play the drums and ukulele, and later touring with various Entertainments National Service Association (ENSA) companies and bands, until soon after his eighteenth birthday in September 1943, when he was called up for military service. As he spent much of his childhood touring the country with his parents, he had few roots, but his RAF posting was the first time he had been separated from his family.

. . . .

When the time came to report for medical assessment, his eyesight was found to be too poor for him to become a pilot and he seemed condemned to the tedium of ground duties, until he saw a poster inviting recruits with theatrical skills to audition for an RAF concert party known as the 'Gang Show'. It was a chance encounter that was to be decisive. He found himself in the company of a generation of men, many of whom went on to perform with distinction in all fields of showbusiness, and it was his good fortune that his life spanned an age of rapid development in the media of radio, television, recording and film, in all of which he contributed work of the highest calibre. The schoolboy hero Bluebottle, from the BBC radio comedy *The Goon Show*, was just one of many characters he brought vividly to life.

The role of the RAF Gang Shows as a catalyst for the growth of British light entertainment in the second half of the twentieth century can be deduced from the names of some of those who took part: Tony Hancock, Dick Emery, Graham Stark, Frank Thornton, David Lodge and Douglas 'Cardew' Robinson, among others. Peter Sellers may have been the most talented of them all, but it seems that this was not particularly apparent at the start of his RAF career. He is reported to have been rather shy and self-effacing, but he soon came to realise that he could overcome this by taking on the voices and mannerisms of other people, both real and imagined. This gift for shape-shifting would come to define his whole life.

After auditioning to the RAF's impresario, Ralph Reader, he was absorbed into the Gang Show family and began by touring air force bases around Britain, before being posted to South-East Asia. This must have been like taking a gap year and going to university all at once – leaving home and travelling to the far side of the world, while at the same time receiving a thorough grounding in the practicalities of show business under extreme conditions, in the midst of a global conflict. Far from being daunting, the war represented, for Sellers, a life-changing opportunity. This book reveals previously unknown film footage, recordings and radio broadcasts, as well as records of over a hundred performances across two continents. It charts his progress from raw recruit to Gang Show veteran, a journey full of colour and inspiration – a formative experience indeed.

What follows is the story of one young man and his rather unorthodox war.

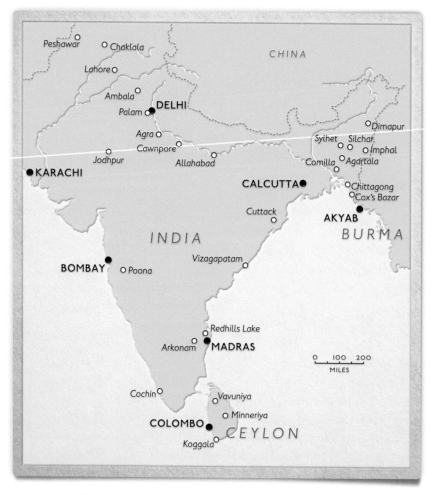

Map of some of the larger Allied air bases in India and Ceylon.

Chapter I:

OVERTURE

As Britain declares war with Germany on 3 September 1939, Peter Sellers is five days short of his fourteenth birthday. He is living with his mother Agnes ('Peg') in a small terraced cottage in Muswell Hill Road, north London. Previous biographers have reported that she runs an antique shop, or that she is in the business of buying and selling gold and silver trinkets. Meanwhile Peter's father William ('Bill') Sellers, a pianist, is apparently resident elsewhere, when not on tour with one performing company or another. The electoral roll of 1938 shows both Bill and Peg at no.1 Roydon Mansions, an apartment just off what is now the Archway Roundabout. Peter is a pupil at St Aloysius' College, which is roughly half way between the two addresses. He is an only child and a rather solitary one, but he enjoys listening to the radio and sometimes imitates the voices of the stars of the period, for the amusement of a schoolmate. He plays cricket and helps his mother with her wheeling and dealing. For a while life goes on in relative normality, but the war obtrudes as the bombing offensive against London begins. There is a plan to evacuate the boys of St Aloysius' school to Cambridgeshire; Peg, however, decides to take matters into her own hands. The family (Bill included) pack up and leave London for the town of Ilfracombe, on the north Devon coast, where one of Peg's cousins is manager of a theatre. Peter never goes to school again. He helps out at the theatre

Performing in ENSA, probably with his father at the piano.

Advertisement in *The Stage*, 6 November 1941.

(starting in the usual way, by sweeping the stage), and eventually moves on to lighting and other backstage and front-of-house tasks. Meanwhile, his father is teaching him to play the ukulele, he wins a talent competition doing comic impressions in a double act with his friend Derek Altman and he is inspired by a visiting jazz orchestra to take up the drums. He shows considerable talent for this and, after his mother pays for lessons, is soon sitting in with local bands. He and Bill sign up with the Entertainments National Service Association (ENSA), which was established by the actor/ directors Basil Dean and Leslie Henson in 1939 to organise entertainment for the armed forces, employing civilians from every branch of the performing arts, from ballet dancers to circus acts. They begin travelling around the country performing musical numbers and variety turns, which seem to have included some early attempts at impressions by Peter.

Eventually, he is separated professionally from his father and spends some time as the drummer in a troupe with the rather startling title of 'Waldini & his Gypsy Band' (actually fronted by a Welshman whose real name is Wally Bishop), first on the bandstands in

RAF recruiting poster.

Ilfracombe and subsequently on the road, under the auspices of ENSA. Touring conditions are grim; they have to endure being billeted, among other places, on the premises of a provincial undertaker.

He is ambitious (or at least, his mother is, on his behalf): the advertisement opposite appears in the trade paper *The Stage* on 6 November 1941. The 'young ultra-modern swing drummer' is only sixteen, but he already has professional experience, and is hungry for more.

Meanwhile, the time is coming closer when he will have to play his part in the war proper; all young men are to be called up for service. Some accounts say that he volunteers for the Royal Air Force, while others imply that he is conscripted. Both these propositions are

. . . .

13

likely to be true; given the inevitability of enlistment, volunteering to fly will mean that he is not randomly assigned to one of the other services. Upon turning eighteen, he will discover what the Air Force has in mind for him.

By the summer of 1943 Peter and his mother are in Brighton where he has found work drumming with a local band at the Regent Dance Hall, while awaiting his call-up. They are renting accommodation in Ross Mansions, Middle Street. Coincidentally, the actor and director Bryan Forbes also describes lodging there during the immediate post-war years; it is dilapidated and squalid. Peter's official notification to join up with the RAF arrives at the end of the year. For the foreseeable future, his life as a civilian is over.

Peter's service record shows that he is ordered to report to the Aviation Candidates Selection Board at Birmingham on 19 December 1943. He is now officially the property of the RAF; he is promptly sent home 'on reserve' to await his posting. This comes in January 1944. He is bound for No.2 Recruits Centre at Cardington, and thence for Basic Training.

Basic Training

For the next four or five weeks Peter, along with all other new recruits, undergoes a training regime designed to accustom young men from a wide range of social backgrounds to service discipline. In practice, this means obsessive attention to the details of uniform, physical fitness, marching and drilling and other repetitive menial tasks, as well as handling weapons and other equipment. It must seem as though they will never get anywhere near an actual aeroplane. Peter, who is used to being treated like an adult by his family, probably finds all this a considerable shock. He has already

Opposite: Portrait of Peter wearing khaki drill uniform, c.1944.

gained a reputation for mischief whilst on tour with ENSA groups. He later tells chat-show host Simon Dee: 'I was a bit of a tearaway in those days.'[1] There are tales, possibly apocryphal, that his theatrical connections enable him to organise visits from well-known entertainers to the various bases on which he finds himself; also that he is sent food parcels by his mother to top up the uninspiring rations. At any rate, we can guess that he finds his RAF adventure not as exciting or glamorous as he supposed it would be. And with the news that he has failed his medical on account of his short-sightedness, things look bleaker still. Fortunately, however, matters are about to take an unexpected turn for the better.

Ralph Reader and the Gang Shows

The British armed forces of the Second World War took entertainment very seriously. They recognised that large numbers of men, posted far away from home, exposed to serious danger and often miserable conditions, needed to be kept occupied and amused when off-duty. Whilst ENSA was sending civilian artistes to the front line, the services each also had their own official concert parties. In the RAF, these were under the supervision of Ralph Reader, impresario of the Boy Scout Gang Shows in the 1930s. Born in Somerset, he had travelled to America in his twenties and worked as a singer, dancer and choreographer on Broadway, and on his return to the UK became instrumental in producing the popular variety shows given by massed groups of Scouts.

The idea for the RAF Shows came from a conversation between Reader, then a Squadron Leader in RAF Intelligence, and a friend, Air Commodore Archie Boyle, who told him of his concerns about welfare on RAF stations, especially those in remote areas. Boyle thought that a group of entertainers visiting the bases could have a dual function – to boost morale and also report back on any developing discontent. In 1939 he first asked Reader to put together some men and produce a show to tour. Reader decided to enlist the

help of some former Scout Gang Show performers, but he insisted
that they be serving in the Air Force (some of them had to be
hurriedly called up), to ensure they were distinct from the civilian
ENSA parties already doing the rounds. He accompanied some of
the first Gang Shows on tour, observing their effect on audiences
and keeping his eyes and ears open for signs of unrest or sedition. He
only remembered one incident, when in France he witnessed a girl,
working in a cafe, passing coded messages to German agents. He
reported the occurrence and recalled: 'She was shot as a spy.'[2]

If all this seems a bit far-fetched, *Boys' Own* stuff, that's because
it is. The shows' improbable undercover mission rapidly became
irrelevant, subsumed by their success in their other purpose: to raise
the airmen's spirits. The RAF shows simply proved themselves to
be first-rate entertainments. In a world before television, and when
mail to those serving overseas could take weeks or even months to
arrive, it's hard to overstate the importance of an evening out at the
theatre or cinema to these men. The Gang Shows were attached to
the newly-formed Department of Air Force Welfare, which was
concerned with all non-combatant aspects of service life. DAFW
(section 4) based itself at Houghton Street, Aldwych, in premises
vacated by the London School of Economics, which had evacuated
to Cambridge. Usefully, the building had a small theatre onsite.
Welfare then set about increasing the number of its touring shows by
seeking out talent amongst the lower ranks of the force.

Reader and his team were only allowed to recruit men who
were not aircrew and who did not have particular expertise in
engineering or any other skills vital to the war effort. However,
their advertisements in RAF magazines and on bases were explicit:
experience in show business was essential. By 1944 Gang Shows had
travelled throughout the UK, Italy, North Africa and the Far East.
One show even appeared at RAF Kaldadarnes in Iceland. From
their formation up to the end of the war, fifteen numbered shows
had travelled over 350,000 miles worldwide. There was an emphasis

on visiting the remotest outposts possible, many of which received no other forms of live entertainment and where the conditions precluded ENSA from sending civilians. (At least, this was the theory; by 1944 ENSA parties were also following close behind the troops on the front line, and Britain's best-known wartime entertainer, Vera Lynn, had travelled all the way to Burma, where she insisted on experiencing, at first-hand, the hardships of the tropics and the jungle.) Life for the Gang Shows wasn't exactly dangerous, but it could be quite challenging. Gang Show no.1 travelled to France in July 1944, just six weeks after D-Day. This party included Dick Emery. They were followed in mid-August by GS5, with Cardew Robinson and accompanied by Reader. They were accidentally shot at by a passing friendly aircraft during their performance, causing Robinson to improvise: 'We're not that bad, are we??'[3]

Peter Sellers seems to have encountered Reader in March or early April 1944 during one of the Squadron Leader's visits to bases in search of more manpower. Peter has finished his basic training and is stationed somewhere in the UK on ground duties and not much enthused by whatever it is he is supposed to be doing. Reader tells the story: the young man responded to a notice inviting interested parties to audition, claiming to be a drummer who also did a few impressions: 'I can do some bits from *ITMA*' (a popular wartime radio programme, 'It's That Man Again' i.e. Adolf Hitler). Reader made an appointment to hear him the following morning at the NAAFI theatre, and upon his arrival behind the stage, he came across Peter entertaining some men who had been sweeping out the hall with an impersonation of Reader himself 'singing *Riding Along on the Crest of a Wave** even worse than I sing it'[4]. It's easy to imagine the sudden tension among the audience, who can see what Peter

---

*the Gang Show theme song, written by Reader for his Scout shows. It was sung at every performance by the RAF Gang Shows. They also had a distinctive backcloth, which was always hung, no matter how improvised the staging.

. . . .

can't; the slightly queasy moment when the aspiring performer turns round; and the rapid recovery to pose the question 'Well Sir, do I get jankers, or are you thirsty?' Even then, Peter's nerve is strong. And apparently, Reader is thirsty.

Things probably move quite swiftly now. Peter is transferred from his ground duties to the Entertainment Unit, attached to the Air Ministry in London. There he joins nine others to form Gang Show no.10, a mix of experienced veterans of earlier shows, and some newcomers like himself.

The cast of characters who form No.10. Gang Show in 1944 are:

Dudley Jones (*Sergeant in charge*): a classically trained actor and singer who joined the RAF Gang Shows in 1940. Known as "The Pocket Caruso" because of his excellent tenor voice, he was previously in shows including GS7.

Wally Sparks (*Sergeant*): a comedian who had worked with Reader on the original pre-war Scout Gang Shows, from their very beginnings in 1932.

James Patton Elliott (*Sergeant*): a comedian from Rotherham whose act, as Gene Patton, was *The Whistling Comic*. His four sons followed him into showbusiness: two of them became the children's entertainers known as 'The Chuckle Brothers'.

Norrie Paramor: a pianist, later to become renowned as a record producer, arranger and band-leader. He was replaced before the group left the UK by:

Maurice Arnold: pianist/accordionist who had played in dance bands in Manchester, featured in four Royal Command Performances, and regularly broadcast for the BBC.

Gang Show no.10 in the theatre at Houghton Street, 1944.

L to R: Jones, Kane, Osborne, Wilkie, Elliott, Sparks, Arnold, Sellers, Harry Whitney, Taylor, unknown.

George ("*G.F.X.*") Taylor: a Scottish comedian whose act was *A Breath o'th' Heather,* 'enjoyed by Sassenach and Scot alike'[5].

Les Osborne: a clarinet and saxophone player from Liverpool who was once a part of Harry Korris's *Happidrome* (a popular pre-war variety show) and played with Harry Leader's Band.

Harry Kane: an actor and violin player, once of the *Three Aristocrats* show, and brother of a well-known dance band singer, Alan Kane.

Ben Novak: an acrobat who had been 'Roli' in a duo, *Roli & Poli,* in Bob Fossett's Circus. He replaced Harry Whitney before the show left England.

Bill Wilkie: an accordion player from Perth in Scotland. Peter got on particularly well with Bill, giving him the nickname 'Tottie Wee' partly for his diminutive figure and also with a nod to his fondness for a wee tot of Scotch whisky. Wilkie often told this story: on being asked, as a raw recruit, to pointlessly paint a pile of stones white, he replied '… I could set up a concert party, run your dance band, get the troops singing, and what do you do? Give me some stones to paint. A total waste of manpower.'[6] His plea earned him an audition for Reader, and a rapid redeployment, with his squeeze-box, to Houghton Street.

The casts of the shows would often change at the last minute, usually because one of the members failed a medical, or was unable to travel owing to family circumstances.

There is a three-week rehearsal period, during which they develop their programme. Reader writes most of the material, using the talents available in each particular grouping. Some of the sketches are adapted from his scripts for the Scout Gang Shows. He insists, quaintly if viewed from today's perspective, that they keep the comedy clean, preferring humorous or ironic takes on service situations, familiar to the men who will be their audiences. Again, he wants the Gang Shows to set themselves apart from ENSA productions, some of which are reported to be rather risqué, besides lacking much common ground with those they are supposed to entertain. Naughtiness in the ENSA ranks sometimes extended to off-stage activities too. An exasperated telegram sent by one of their tour managers to the Officer Commanding in Calcutta complained that 'Sergeant Hall travelled in same sleeping berth with Miss Barrie last night, ignoring my orders.'[7]

Peter and co. are soon ready to launch their show, with a performance on 30 May 1944 in front of senior Air Ministry staff at the Houghton Street theatre, followed by visits to bases further afield in England. Some writers have stated that GS10 plays at stations as far north as the Hebrides, Orkneys and Shetland Islands during this time, but there is a lack of evidence to support this. A programme from one of their later concerts may be the reason for the assumption – its Introduction includes the following detail: 'The show you are about to see is No.10 unit, whose members ... have toured all over Great Britain, Northern Ireland, the Orkneys and Shetlands.'[8] Dudley Jones remembers spending five weeks in Ireland whilst with a previous party, so this almost certainly doesn't refer to GS10 collectively.

In any case, they know that it won't be long before they receive a posting overseas where their work is most needed. Bill Wilkie takes a short spell of leave, during which he gets married; the other Scotsman in the show, George Taylor, acts as his best man. Then their preparations continue. A formidable cocktail of vaccinations against every tropical disease that they could conceivably encounter makes them feel terribly sick and brings home to them forcibly that the relatively comfortable time they've so far enjoyed is coming to an end. They are about to begin a remarkable journey, one which would be beyond the means and imagination of most young men of their generation, were it not for the circumstances of war.

. . . .

Chapter 2:

ON THE ROAD

O n 7 July 1944, RAF Gang Show no.10 is posted to No.5 Personnel Despatch Centre at Blackpool. This takes them to the epicentre of showbusiness in the north of England; the town's many theatres, cinemas and dance halls are flourishing just as in peacetime. It's familiar to Peter, of course, from his time there drumming with bands. It is also overflowing with service personnel, so there is a constant captive audience. 5 PDC is

Postcard of the Brighton Hydro Hotel, Blackpool.

headquartered at the Brighton Hydro Hotel on South Shore (now the Colonial Hotel).

By now they probably know their destination: South East Asia Command. There are a great many RAF bases in India which has been under severe threat from the Japanese. The force has been engaged in transporting and supplying troops in the forward areas of Burma, as well as providing air cover for operations in the region. Supporting the aircrew are thousands of ground staff – construction, maintenance, repair and salvage units, provisions and stores, communication, observation and radar posts, air/sea rescue, and more. ENSA parties are regularly travelling there, as well as two Gang Shows (nos. 4 and 6), but more entertainment is desperately needed for men thousands of miles from home who are working in conditions utterly alien to them and sometimes very harsh. Among the difficulties are the monsoon rains between June and August; the extreme heat and humidity; dangerous animals and insects; the most basic living conditions and often restricted supplies of equipment and provisions. A film produced by the Air Ministry in 1945, *Life in Air Command South East Asia*, attempts to prepare those posted there for what they will experience, but it glosses over some of the less appealing aspects in favour of a 'see the world'-style travelogue. It's ironic that by the time this film is put together, the war in Europe is almost at an end, but it is still going on in Asia, where the troops have often been dubbed the 'Forgotten Army'. However, there is no doubt that for most servicemen and women, their time in the Far East is an unforgettable experience, as much positive as negative. One advantage, at least in the larger camps near cities, is the availability of exotic fruit and a wider range of foods in general than has been seen in Britain since the start of the war. There is also cheap Indian labour to provide services like laundry (*dhobi*), refreshments (*char* = tea), tailoring (*darzi*), and barbering.

A performance for an RAF audience in Blackpool has been arranged for GS10. Their final warm-up before departing on their tour of duty is on 11 July in a small theatre within the large and imposing store of the Blackpool Co-operative Society. The BCS Jubilee Theatre hosts regular RAF entertainments during this period, including one on 6 June 1944 – D-Day! – a show by Gang Show no. 9, among whose members is Tony Hancock. They are about to tour Italy and North Africa. GS10's programme (*below*) shows that Maurice Arnold has replaced Norrie Paramor on the piano, and Peter has amended his billing to 'DRUMS & Impersonations'. Later, in the barren period pre- and post-demob, when he's trying to get noticed in London, he will use a similar tag line on his business cards.

The 'Surprise Item' at the end of the performance may well be a jam session by a sub-set of GS10. Maurice Arnold, Les Osborne, Bill Wilkie, Harry Kane and Peter have formed a quintet which they initially call *Just Five*. This is an extremely proficient little band and its sets will become a particular highlight of GS10's shows.

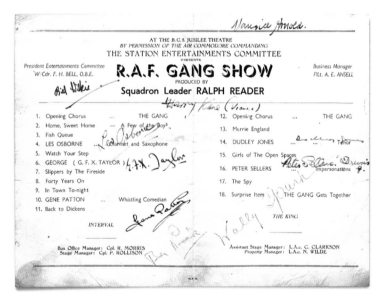

Autographed programme from the BCS Jubilee Theatre, 11 July 1944.

'Just Five' quintet from Gang Show no. 10. Peter was good at sewing, and he added padding inside the shoulders to give the shirts a crisper outline.

Eastwards on the SS *Mooltan*

The SS *Mooltan* was built in 1923 by Harland & Wolff for the Peninsular & Oriental Company. She had been used on the route to Australia until 1939 when she was requisitioned by the War Office, first as a cruiser, and then for troop convoys. In October/November 1942, she took part in Operation Torch, transporting US Army troops to North Africa. By the time Peter and his colleagues join over 4,000 others on board bound for India, she has been re-fitted, losing much of her luxurious interior. Men below officer rank would sleep in bunks or hammocks, at uncomfortably close quarters with their neighbours. As the voyage progresses and the weather becomes warmer, some resort to sleeping up on deck, under the open sky.

They sail from Liverpool on 18 July 1944. Access to the Suez Canal having been restored in the spring of 1943, their route takes them through the Mediterranean to Port Said. Previously, convoys have

SS *Mooltan* in the Suez Canal, with troops taking a swim.

been forced to take the long way round, via the southern tip of Africa, stopping over at Durban. During the voyage, they are rehearsing and, apparently, giving evening performances in the Officers' Mess. 'Such was the heat that an army of volunteers was required to dry shirts etc.'[9] Musicians like Bill Wilkie are also drafted in to play for religious services on board. They reach Suez on 1 August, staying there until the fourth, and then pass via Aden to Bombay, arriving on 14 August.

RAF records from this period survive in varying levels of completeness. All stations or bases, and units, made regular entries in a local document known as the Operations Record Book (ORB). This consisted of Form 540, the summary of events, and Form 541, the record of events. Form 541 often listed flying or working activity by the hour; Form 540 might be set out as a daily diary of occurrences, or sometimes it was formatted in categories with a digest of each one (operations, medical, welfare, etc.). In each case, one officer seems to have been responsible for collating and writing up the log. It is in Form 540 that reports of entertainment and recreation can be found. For the RAF in India, these logs, where they still exist, are often highly detailed and informative. Unfortunately, many are lost, some owing to incidents of freak weather or fires on the bases. But what the remaining books demonstrate is that the visit of a Gang Show (or ENSA party), amid the dull routine, was sufficiently unusual and exciting to be noted, and the compiler often gave additional, colourful descriptions of the event. Interestingly, this was clearly more prevalent the further from the UK it took place. There was an obsession with noting the minutiae of life in the service overseas – if it moved or spoke, it was recorded. This may have been due to a combination of British bureaucracy and simple boredom (this is especially true in the case of ground-based units – the flying squadrons probably had plenty of excitement!). For the modern reader, these books can be unexpectedly entertaining.

Les Osborne, Peter, and Maurice Arnold, in August 1944, just arrived in India and enjoying an almost forgotten pleasure. Bananas are a familiar sight in photos from forces in the Far East, but have become a distant memory back home.

Arrival in India

August 1944

On approaching the harbour in Bombay, the impressive sight that greets arriving personnel is the famous archway known as the 'Gateway of India'. They are disembarked, witnessing for the first time the mixture of splendour and squalor typical of Indian cities at the time: the heat and dust, the sounds, the colours, the smells. The previously mentioned Air Ministry information film *Life in ACSEA* warns against being approached by beggars and street traders. The first thing most of the men do is stop by the uniform stores to exchange their large and old-fashioned *topee* hats for more practical wide-brimmed bush hats. Their initial destination is the Base Reception Depot at Worli, where they will await their first orders. In the case of the Gang Show, we can assume that they have a period of acclimatisation, probably a bit more rehearsal, and then, on 21 August, they are assigned to tour the stations in 227 Group. On 25 August the Operations Record Book for RAF Santa Cruz, on the outskirts of Bombay, reports:

25th / 20.30 *No.4 R.A.F. Gang Show gave their first performance in India in the airmen's dining hall of the new camp*
26th / 20.30 *No.10 R.A.F. Gang Show gave a performance in the airmen's dining hall*

This immediately presents a conundrum. GS4 has already been on tour in India since June 1944, in the hills of the northwest frontier, then entertaining the leave parties at Solan before travelling eastwards to Assam and into Burma. Among their party is AC1 Graham Stark, later to become a close friend of Peter's. It seems likely that the compiler of the record has confused the numbers of the two shows which appear on consecutive nights.

The station magazine, *Ariel*, of the RAF camp at Sion (an area of Bombay not far from Santa Cruz) carries a review of GS10 dated

Friday 25 August (noted as 'pay day' so spirits must have been high). 'Versatile Peter Seller [sic] knocks off the flim-flams and paradiddles on the drums like a Krupa* … and is a better-than-average impressionist to boot … this was our first Gang here, they were good.'

So the 'new camp' referred to in the Santa Cruz ORB seems to be down the road at Sion, where, thanks to their proximity to Worli, they boast of often hosting the Indian debuts of visiting companies.

GS4 and GS10 clearly do not meet at Santa Cruz – Stark says that he first encounters Peter in London at the Houghton Street HQ in the spring of 1946 – so that also suggests separate venues. GS10 have probably left the morning after their performance – they are headed for the Punjab, and thence to the northwest frontier.

Dudley Jones, interviewed by Richard Fawkes for his book *Fighting for a Laugh*, gives an insight into their schedule:

> *As a rule when we arrived on a station we did a show that night. If you left it any longer than that, they did ask, who are these chaps who stay in bed until 10am, but once you'd done the show, it's like the telly now – 'Oh, saw you last night mate, marvellous.'*[10]

September 1944

The next entry in the records shows them at Ambala on 5 September: 'R.A.F. Gang Show at 2100 Hours. Performed before a full house & was very much appreciated by all.' They are up in the high country now, towards the hill stations, and with autumn approaching, the climate is rather different to that in Bombay. Bill Wilkie mentions conditions at Upper Topa, in the Murree Hills, where the cold is so extreme that containers of hair oil freeze, only thawing on descent to

---

*Gene Krupa (1909–73) – a well-known American jazz drummer and band leader, associated with, among others, Benny Goodman. In the immediate post-war years, Peter's drumming act was sometimes billed as 'Britain's answer to Gene Krupa'.

a lower altitude, upon which the jars crack, and disgorge their greasy contents into his kit bag.

They are at RAF Risalpur, near Nowshera, on 14 and 15 September – 'two excellent performances' – and in the Garrison Theatre in Peshawar four days later, from where the show is broadcast on radio. These transmissions are probably organised locally by RAF Welfare, to give the performances a wider reach. Their visit to Samungli and Quetta lasts five days. On 22 September, they are flown by 31 Squadron to Samungli:

> *Arrival of Dakota aircraft from Basal, bringing No.10 RAF Gang Show. It was generally considered by the R.A.F. personnel that this was one of the best entertainments seen in this country … they were a great success and very much appreciated.*

Gang Show no.10 on board a Dakota transport aircraft.

The Dakotas, some of them extremely old, are the workhorses of the RAF in India. Often they are doorless: Bill Wilkie remembers ' … one would be sitting on a prop basket looking into space as the aircraft hedge-hopped over the jungle.'[11] The IWM film shows a few moments of GS10's flight in the bare belly of one of these planes, crammed in amongst all their gear, laughing and waving to the cameraman. However, they depart Quetta by train; next stop: Karachi.

October 1944

Their destination in Karachi is the RAF station at Drigh Road.

'September 29th, 30th, October 2nd: 'RAF Gang Show No.10 gave successful and greatly appreciated show in Airmen's Theatre'.

The larger bases adjacent to towns and cities are clearly better equipped for entertainment. Theatres have been adapted from existing civilian buildings or rigged up in Messes and canteens. GS10 is preceded at Drigh Road by the Karachi Amateur Light Opera Company's presentation of Gilbert & Sullivan's *HMS Pinafore*! There are also greater numbers of men on these stations, hence the longer visits (and they often give two shows in one day).

Despite the punishing schedule, there is still time to visit the city of Karachi. Bill Wilkie remembers that he and Peter, who by now have become good friends, are out on the town one night and have managed to miss the last transport back to base. They have no choice but to walk. Peter decides to tell a few ghost stories (he is fond of doing this) so they are already spooked when they encounter a procession of wailing locals parading through the streets with flaming torches bearing an uncovered corpse on a litter. A surprising turn of speed is shown by our heroes as they flee the alarming tableau. Funerals are very different in this part of the world.

The beginning of October finds them by the coast, on the flying-boat base at Korangi Creek. The station magazine, *Boost*, reports that after their cinema has been put out of action by the monsoon, an open-air screen and stage is set up in the outdoor gym, and dubbed the *Korangi Pallandium* [sic], 'The Cinema with the Big Roof'. They are doing well for films, but the arrival of GS10 is a rare treat. The performance is given 'in good conditions … to large and delighted audiences':

> *Hitting the Creek near the beginning of a nine months tour, Ralph Reader's No.10 Gang Show provided film-satiated Creekites with a real flesh-and-blood show … Entertainments such as these are a grand tonic for the lads, whose visits to the 'live' theatre … are now fading memories.*

These station magazines are another surprising discovery from the archives. Professionally printed, usually in nearby towns, they contain not only information on the area, reports of sports and entertainment

Victory edition of Boost magazine,
RAF Korangi Creek, 1945.

and practical advice, but also original stories, poems and cartoons penned by men from the units, and occasional black and white photographs of female film stars! Their covers bear distinctive designs, often in colour, but the rest of the contents are produced on low grade paper, which helps to make them light enough for the men to send home by post if they want to. The whole enterprise is organised by local Welfare officers.

Boost, in a Victory edition of 1945, has a dig at some other visiting artistes: George Formby and Joyce Grenfell 'were enthusiastically received, as were the amazingly versatile, clever and entertaining R.A.F. Gang Shows', but 'there were also a few ENSA shows (not so versatile, not so clever and not so entertaining) … there was a general query as to what many of them did before the war, and what they will do … now that the war is over!'. Whereas, everywhere they go, the Gang Shows are building a reputation for slick, high-quality, crowd-pleasing fare.

Peter and GS10 are now headed west, to Jiwani, one of the staging posts on pre-war British Empire flying routes. It is now an RAF stop-off point for all manner of air transport. On 9 October:

Group photo of Gang Show no. 10 prior to a performance in India.

. . . .

A Dakota from Mauripur brought No.10 Gang Show, and a performance was given in the evening attended by some 180/200 personnel (including Americans and B.O.A.C.) This was the first stage show that has visited this unit for many months and was highly appreciated by all ranks.

These brief reviews show that the Gang Shows are being deliberately sent to the more distant stations, bringing music and laughter to hard-working men who might otherwise feel almost forgotten.

Jodhpur

The Maharajah of Jodhpur was a great friend to the many servicemen stationed in the region. He held the rank of Honorary Air Commodore and regularly opened his vast palace and its grounds to the forces and their families. Then called the Chittar Palace because of the distinctive pink stone from Chittar Hill used in its construction, it is now known as Umaid Bhawan. It was built by the Maharajah between 1929 and 1943 and is still occupied by his descendants. Parts of it are open to the public, as a museum and a hotel. At Christmas 1943 he gave a lavish garden party for British forces, with a buffet, dancing and swimming in the pools. He also offered temporary accommodation to the men of RAF Jodhpur when their billets were flooded during the monsoon. Within the Palace was the Maharajah's private theatre, the scene of GS10's next big adventure.

13.10.44)   *S/LDR.RALPH READER'S GANG SHOW visited*
14.10.44)   *JODHPUR and gave four shows at the CHITTAR*
               PALACE, kindly loaned by AIR COMMODORE
               HIS HIGHNESS THE MAHARAJAH OF
               JODHPUR. HIS HIGHNESS accompanied by the
               MINISTER IN WAITING attended the performance
               on 14.10.44.

Camp Chronicle, RAF Jodhpur's monthly magazine, carries a review:

There wasn't a dull moment throughout the show, and some of the acts were really outstanding. The high spot of the evening … was the "Session" by the band comprising of piano, drums, sax, clarinet, fiddle, and piano-accordian [sic]. The drummer was really 'solid' and he certainly was no newcomer to the 'skins'. The pianist had a nice style … the sax player was excellent and knew his gen on extemporisation. The violin player was very pleasant to listen to and the same can be said of the accordian player … It was a very good show, well put over, and well worth seeing.

. . . .

The *Just Five Quintet* has established itself by this stage as a feature of GS10's programme. In Jodhpur, Maurice Arnold plays an arrangement of the *Warsaw Concerto* by Richard Addinsell (from the 1941 film *Dangerous Moonlight*), and Bill Wilkie chooses *In The Mood* for his solo. These pieces, so familiar to audiences today, are of course relatively new and on-trend in 1944.

From Jodhpur, they head north-east, via Delhi to Cawnpore, playing at the Fox Cinema on 20 and 21 October, followed by stations at Chakheri, Allahabad ('a very excellent entertainment … much appreciated by all ranks'), and Phaphamau – about half way between Cawnpore and Benares. Here they perform to 352 Maintenance Unit in an aircraft hangar which is filled to capacity.

In addition to the long sea voyage to India and the regular flights in ageing Dakotas, the Gang Show's main means of transport over such huge distances is the Indian Railways. Thousands of troops

---

<table>
<tr><td colspan="3">See instructions for use of this form in K. R. and
A. C. I. and notes in R. A. F. Field Service
Pocket Book.</td><td>OPERATIONS RECORD BOOK
of (Unit or Formation) No. 352 Maintenance Unit, R.A.F.,
INDIA.</td><td>Air Force (India) Form
No. of pages used for day month b
Page.........3</td></tr>
</table>

Place.	Date.	Time.	Summary of Events.	References to Appendices
PHAPHAMAU.	26.10.44.		Wing Commander L. SCULLARD, M.B.E., returned from 230 Group by air and resumed command. Squadron Leader COOK(Equip), 230 Group visited the Unit in connection with Equipment Policy at A.S.U's.	
	27.10.44.		A concert was given by No. 10 R.A.F. Gang Show in No. 15 Hangar. 80% of the Unit attended and the hangar was filled to capacity. The C.O., on behalf of the Unit, afterwards thanked the artists for the entertainment they had given.	
	30.10.44.		Notification was received that 227 Group took over administration services from 226 Group wef. 1st November, 1944.	
	31.10.44.		Squadron Leader COOK, 230 Group, returned by air.	
			GENERAL. Large increase of production this month, 99 aircraft actually being produced, i.e. 47 Twin Engined Aircraft. 52 Multi Engined Aircraft. Approximately 250 incoming and outgoing aircraft were handled.	
			DOMESTIC CAMP POSITION AND WELFARE. Considerable difficulties are being experienced in connection with the feeding of personnel due to:-	
			(a) The cookhouse being inadequate for this purpose having been built to cater for 350 people in one small kitchen and 3 dining rooms.	
			(b) The smallness of the dining rooms causes a considerable amount of congestion and rush, e.g., breakfast and dinner, although the camp is split into 2 working shifts with half an hour lag.	
			(c) Insufficient personnel in cookhouses.	
			(d) Quality of rations generally poor and still not entirely adequate.	

can be efficiently moved around the continent in this way, but the conditions on board are the opposite of luxurious. There are hard benches to sit or sleep on (most journeys take days rather than hours), a small burner for heating water to make tea, and a hole in the floor is the only toilet facility. According to Graham Stark, air-conditioning is sometimes provided by suspending a block of ice from the ceiling of the carriage. Dudley Jones remembers: 'Any station you stop at, in the middle of the desert where there's nothing to be seen for miles, as soon as the train stops, from the bowels of the earth there'd appear four million people with tea things and cakes and the lot.'[12] Carriages may be reserved for service personnel, but this is often disregarded by the locals, who climb into or onto every spare inch of space. Peter and Ben Novak deal with this in an

Opposite: Extract from the Operations Record Book of 352 Maintenance Unit, October 1944. They have enjoyed the Gang Show, but difficulties with catering and rations are adversely affecting morale.

Above: Peter and Ben Novak dancing; Bill Wilkie on accordion.

. . . .

inventive manner. While the rest of the party goes for refreshments, they stand on the steps up to the train door and pretend to have a fierce quarrel in a non-existent, quasi-Indian language, which causes everyone to give them a very wide berth. (Dudley Jones believed that Peter's subsequent impersonations of Indian characters on radio and in film had their origins in this ruse.)

Here it is evident that Peter is continuing to develop the strong performing personality so characteristic of his early career, as well as displaying a subversive sense of humour that will mesh perfectly with that of Spike Milligan. For many serving men, satire seems to have become a strategy for processing their experiences. But Peter's war (unlike that of his fellow Goons, Milligan and Secombe, both of whom are in the Army) is short on danger and direct action, something of which he will always be conscious. For him, the war is a liberating experience, full of masquerade and mischief.

November 1944

At the beginning of November, the next part of GS10's tour begins, as they move on to West Bengal. The first mention of them here is on 2 November when they arrive at Baigachi, some way north of Calcutta. The ORB for the station maintains that space in their cinema is thought to be too limited for the expected numbers attending. Accordingly it is decided to put on the show in the open air, on a specially built stage at the other side of the airfield: ' … an aircraft blast pen was selected for the purpose.' Dudley Jones recalls a different scenario – according to him, the cinema is still only half built. 'There was one 100 watt bulb … ' The outdoor stage 'was in fact a boxing ring … they'd taken the posts down … and we'd put a Gang Show backcloth on it.' The performance starts late in the evening, when the temperature starts to fall, though '[it] was about 85 even at night … one never minded playing in the open air.' The footlights are switched on, and an unforeseen hazard arises: ordeal by insects:

> *... not one moth but four million moths ... and praying mantises
> ... mosquitoes and little green [flies]. In fact within two minutes of
> switching the lights on ... the Gang Show letters [on the backcloth]
> were obscured ... and they were so thick in the footlights we could have
> literally shovelled them up.*[13]

After an abortive attempt to start the show, 'covered in creeping
things from head to foot', and unable to speak for fear of swallowing
one, they have to give up. The ORB is restrained in reporting this
calamity: 'when dusk came and the lights were switched on they were
quickly 'blacked out' by millions of green flies. It proved impossible
to overcome this unexpected difficulty'. There is only one thing for
it – everyone and everything must be transported back to the cinema
and that feeble 100w bulb. Half the audience are left outside, and
the ORB adds plaintively 'it is hoped the show will be able to visit
again in the near future.' Sadly, this seems not to have happened, to
everyone's disappointment.

On 5 November, GS10 are entertained to dinner in the
Aircrew House at Base HQ in Calcutta. This could be the occasion,
mentioned by Alexander Walker, on which Peter first meets Denis
Selinger, a theatrical manager and now a gunner in the RAF,
who will become his agent after the war is over. (Also present
is the American actor Melvyn Douglas, in Calcutta overseeing
entertainments for the US Army.) Peter, 'just back from a show in
the jungle'[14], apparently makes friends with Selinger immediately.
But GS10 are soon on the road again, in a south-westerly direction,
appearing in Balasore and Cuttack, and then suffering the indignity
of being almost marooned there. The ORB for RAF Egra, their next
stop, explains:

11th / 2300 *No.10 R.A.F. Gang Show arrives. Late through
failure of B.N.R. [Bengal Nagpur Railway] to attach
their coach to Mail [train] at Cuttack.*

....

Despite the efforts of the RAF administrators in Welfare, their travel arrangements seem prone to such mishaps – more than once, they arrive at a railway station to find that no-one at the next venue knows they are coming. Communications often break down and Dudley Jones remembers the men being on the point of mutiny through sheer frustration. By this stage, the relentless schedule is beginning to take its toll. They are often travelling by day and giving a show each night. During a performance the stage is never empty, with sketches and music following in rapid succession. So many quick changes in rudimentary facilities (sometimes behind a drape 'a foot from where someone was performing'[15]) and the constant, sapping heat leads to exhaustion, and then sickness. At 91 Air Stores Park, Khargpur, on 13 November, the station magazine (the *ASP*) says 'unfortunately a few of the artists were on the sick list and could not appear.' Dudley has to quickly reshuffle the fit personnel: 'You do so-and-so's bit, cut that, and you do something else.'[16]

Peter taking the role of Elizabeth I in the sketch titled *Merrie England*. (Patton is on the left and Les Osborne on the right.) In the version later filmed at Akyab, the Queen is played by George Taylor.

Peter's facility in assuming multiple characters in the blink of an eye surely has its roots here. It's a skill he is later to exploit in several films, such as *The Naked Truth*, *The Mouse that Roared*, and *Dr Strangelove*.

The sickness persists. The show is seen at Salbani on 14 November by Tony Donell, a pilot on Liberators with 356 Squadron. He writes in his diary (transcribed by Mike Jones for the website *Airfields in Midnapore*) 'Went to see RAF concert party held outdoors opposite cinema last night … the show was good, particularly considering that four of the ten of the troupe were away sick.' Two

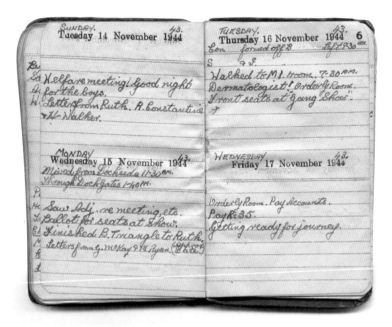

Diary of LAC Thomas Fraser, November 1944. He has written notes from 1943 as well.

days later, LAC Thomas Fraser is in the audience at RAF Digri. He is the lucky winner of front-row seats in a ballot held on the station. His diary (shown here by courtesy of his son Graeme) is far less detailed, with no mention of whether GS10 is still under strength.

It was impossible to escape digestive complaints while serving in this region. The records contain many tales of sudden, violent calls of nature. Graham Stark remembers almost missing an RAF transport flight owing to being unavoidably detained in the facilities. What hurt him most was leaving his precious camera hanging on the back of the toilet door, in his haste to board the aircraft in time.

There is now a gap in the records for GS10, which suggests that this may be the first of two periods of leave which they are allowed during their time in India. These are taken in the hill stations, where the climate is much more pleasant and where European residents take refuge during the hot months. When leave is due, the men are organised into 'Hill Parties' and sent to these rest camps for a week at a time. The Gang Shows may be off duty, but they also entertain others who are already there. Graham Stark has spent a week at Solan with GS4 in June, giving performances to successive Hill Parties, and Dudley Jones also recalls being asked to give a show during their time off – which they do, willingly.

The next recorded appearances of GS10 are on 29 and 30 November in Dhubalia, north of Calcutta, where they get an 'enthusiastic reception'. Here the writer also offers a pithy assessment: 'It appears to be the general opinion that the cleaner a show is, the better it is appreciated.' Once again, the reluctance to resort to smutty humour is noted.

From the listings of the New Empire Theatre, *Calcutta Statesman*, 5 December 1944.

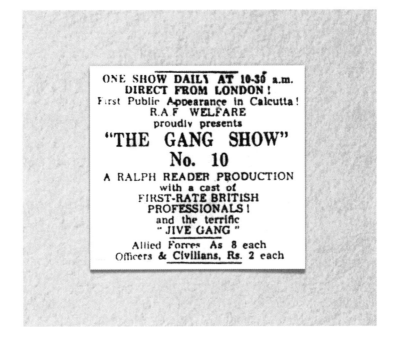

December 1944

They are up early the following day, as on 1 December they begin a week's run at the New Empire Theatre in the heart of Calcutta. This has been heavily promoted in the English-speaking press. The *Calcutta Statesman* contains panel advertisements of increasing detail and anticipation during the preceding week, announcing: 'Direct from London! First public appearance in Calcutta', and promising 'a cast of first-rate British professionals'. Their performances, at 10.30am daily, are open to both civilian and military audiences. There is, unusually, a printed programme for the show, which provides some detail about the performers. 19 year-old Peter is described as 'a boy with

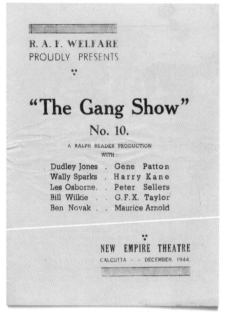

R. A. F. WELFARE
PROUDLY PRESENTS

"The Gang Show"

No. 10.

A RALPH READER PRODUCTION
WITH :

Dudley Jones	Gene Patton
Wally Sparks	Harry Kane
Les Osborne.	Peter Sellers
Bill Wilkie	G.F.X. Taylor
Ben Novak	Maurice Arnold

NEW EMPIRE THEATRE
CALCUTTA - - DECEMBER. 1944.

Programme cover from New Empire Theatre, Calcutta, December 1944.

a future, the baby of the Gang'. The programme is keen to stress that all the men are serving RAF personnel, with no connection to ENSA, and they all receive the same rates of pay as their audiences – there is no special treatment for them.

The magazine of the RAF in Calcutta, *Oasis* (prepared by the Woodpecker Squadron on behalf of Welfare), gives over three pages of its Christmas Number to an article titled simply 'Gang Show'. The magazine has appeared after the festive season, owing to a shortage of labour at the printers', so 'by the time this reaches you the number ten Gang will have dug themselves well into their tour, which is to be an extensive one.' The writer takes to task the minority of servicemen who consider life in the entertainment units to be a soft touch:

The Number Ten Gang Show, reading from left to right, are: Les Osborne, Maurice Arnold, Peter Sellers, Wally Sparks, Gene Patton, Dudley Jones, Bill Wilkie, Ben Novak and Harry Kane.

Group photo from Oasis magazine, Calcutta, Christmas 1944. George Taylor is missing due to illness, which explains Peter having to play the part of Queen Elizabeth. George was in hospital for three months, a casualty of the show's tough schedule.

*I would like to grab one of these sceptics … and drag them into the
Gang Show dressing room, just to show them what hard work really
is. The stage is never unoccupied for a second (Gang Shows do not have
intervals) and each member averages about a dozen appearances; and
in that number … he has probably ten full changes [of] costume and
make-up … The effect to the audience is speed and precision, and that
smooth spontaneity so essential to the success of a show of this type.*

It is certainly no sinecure. He goes on to say that for reasons of
space, it is impossible 'to mention individually the excellence of this
talented company … no artist requires bolstering from another …
each individual is a specialist in his own line … this Gang Show is
superbly good'.

The newspaper advertisements make special mention of the
Just Five quintet, now billed as 'the terrific Jive Gang'. There's a
significance to this, revealed by a surprise entry in the Columbia
Records (India) catalogue for 1946. Under the heading "DANCE
ORCHESTRAS AND BANDS" the following entry appears:

ARNOLD, MAURICE, AND HIS JIVE BOYS
    Come Out, Come Out Wherever You are—Foxtrot ⎫
       (Film: "Step Lively")   ⎬   FB40463
    Doggin' Around—Jive   ⎭

Columbia Records are among several companies who use a recording
studio at Dum Dum, on the outskirts of Calcutta, in close proximity
to the RAF Dum Dum base. Despite the war, there is a busy musical
scene in the city, particularly for jazz singers and bands, whose
universal appeal bridges social and military/civilian divides. So, who are
Maurice Arnold's "Jive Boys"? An educated guess suggests that this is
the *Just Five* quintet making use of a free afternoon or evening during
the first week of December 1944, to spend some time in that studio
laying down these two popular tracks. 'Come out wherever you are' has

recently been sung by Frank Sinatra in the film *Step Lively* (1944). In his book on American popular music in India, Bradley Shope explains:

> *Recorded music from Hollywood films was in high demand ... the availability of imported gramophone discs [was] sharply decreasing because of the war, [so] local performers recorded Hollywood film songs to coincide with a film's debut in Calcutta. Jazz orchestras in the city ... recorded hundreds of these tunes in Calcutta's recording studios.*[17]

The British music newspaper *Melody Maker* confirms this theory: in April 1945, its columnist Jerry Dawson, in his 'Northern News' column, writes that the 'one-time regular Northern broadcaster ... Maurice Arnold ... is currently touring SEAC with one of Ralph Reader's Gang Shows.' He reports that they have travelled over 25,000 miles by land, sea and air, and notes that the jam sessions with the quintet are a feature of the programme, naming the five players. The report ends with the postscript:

> *When in Calcutta last December, the outfit cut a couple of sides for Columbia under the title of Maurice Arnold and his Jive Boys ... [the] record is already on sale in India.*[18]

It's possible that these extramural activities are conducted under the RAF's radar, which could be why there is no mention of it in the name of the band.

Peter has a short drum solo in 'Doggin' Around', which confirms him to be quite accomplished in the style of the time, and he keeps rhythm proficiently enough in 'Come out', without getting in the way of Les Osborne's clarinet and sax riffs, or Harry Kane's violin. Arnold and Wilkie fill in the harmonies. (They seem to have borrowed a string bass player for the session; it is clearly heard in 'Come Out'.)

Centre label from Columbia (India) 78rpm record FB40463. Audio files of both tracks can be found on the website SoundCloud.

Band album with signatures and flamingoes.

There is certainly plenty to do on the regular 'liberty runs' into Calcutta. Men can take a *gharry* (carriage) or *tonga* (a two-wheeled pony cart) to visit the theatre or cinema, and go sightseeing, swimming and dining out at establishments such as the famous 'Firpo's Restaurant & Bar', where there is live jazz and dancing. The Quintet also takes part in a 'Band Gala' at this time, during which they sign a fellow musician's album (*above*). It's most likely that this is in or around the city, prior to their departure for the forward areas. Harry Kane has signed himself "Gloria" – this is his sister's name, so perhaps it has become his nickname within the group. The photograph seems to have been taken in a park or formal garden, possibly at one of the Service Clubs in Calcutta. The photographer is clearly more interested in the flamingoes than the architecture.

. . . .

Chapter 3:

INTO THE JUNGLE

Meanwhile, Graham Stark's Gang Show no.4 has been touring round the southern part of India, including Ceylon, and visiting flying boat bases at Kelai in the Maldive Islands and Cocanada. Finally, they make their way back to Bombay, where they give a show on the brand new stage at the RAF Theatre in Marine Drive. They depart on the SS *Mooltan* on 12 December 1944, leaving GS10 as the only show in India. The *Air Forces Welfare Bulletin* for December notes that 'after a number of performances in Calcutta [GS10] is touring 221 and 224 Groups.' This takes them in a north-easterly direction, towards the Burmese border. Here conditions are not quite as pleasant as they have been until now. The camps are located in wilder, more mountainous areas, where airstrips have been created by clearing trees and other vegetation. Accommodation is of a more temporary kind; the men sleep in huts called *bashas*, made from mud and bamboo with thatched roofs and open sides. Apart from the ever-present mosquitoes, there is the more surreptitious danger of snakes and scorpions. It's advisable to place the legs of a bed into tins of kerosene, to deter the bugs. When eating outdoors, it is vital to be alert for "kite hawks" – birds of prey which will swoop down from a clear blue sky and relieve the unwary of their dinner. This may well consist of the infamous soya link, a sausage substitute reviled by all who are brave enough to taste it.

'The man who said he liked soya links'. Cartoon from *Laugh With SEAC*, 1945.

Spike Milligan, discussing the war with his biographer Dominic Behan, later pictures Peter as 'a lone RAF clerk [sic] ... in Ceylon, imagining he could hear tigers'[19]. Slightly mocking perhaps, yet an evocative idea which suggests that, despite the relative safety of his Gang Show posting, he might still be nervous – everything must just seem so strange. At night, in the open-sided basha, every rustle sounds like the creep of a venomous creature, every far-off rumble might be the conversational growls of enormous cats.

They arrive in Silchar on 11 December where they entertain a number of units at 94 Air Stores Park ('a grand performance ... splendid show'), then visit Kumbhirgram –'an excellent performance putting everyone in a happy mood. We would like to see more shows like this' according to the ORB of 45 Squadron. GS10 seems to have been based at Agartala, from where they are flown by Wing Commander Davy, of 62 Squadron, on a Dakota to Wangjing. They are lucky; after dropping them off, the plane is forced to abort its take-off, as 'smoke started pouring from behind the magneto switch'. Repairs could not be done that day, so the WingCo spent a cold night in the plane and was feared missing by his squadron until they received a message the following morning. There's a large audience at 98 ASP in Wangjing: personnel from all over the area are squeezed into what must have been a sizeable Recreation Room. Likewise, on the following day at Tulihal, 582 members of 906 Wing HQ are entertained. On the succeeding days they are at Tamu, Imphal, Kangla, and Palel. Here they give a farewell show to 909 Wing HQ, who are moving to Kalemyo the following day. The Wing have built an impressive open-air theatre:

> 'The stage was carefully planned in design and lighting and acoustics were all that could be desired. Spacious dressing rooms were built at each side so that the largest touring party could be accommodated.'

This must be a rare luxury for the Gang Show, and the grateful boys 'as always … gave of their best in a clever, witty and varied performance.'

It's Christmas 1944, and Peter is in Agartala and feeling homesick. Years later, he tells the BBC's Michael Parkinson that 'I'd never spent Christmas in a hot country, and I was thinking, my Mum wants me at home'[20]. Sitting on his *charpoy* (an Indian bed made of ropes knotted together) and watching his mates drinking from bottles of the local Rosa Rum, he decides to drown his sorrows in more congenial surroundings. Out comes the costume from the Gang Show wardrobe, the talcum powder to whiten his hair, and off he goes to the Officers' Mess (strictly out-of-bounds to the lower ranks). Fortunately, it is almost empty, apart from one fellow sitting in the corner who is probably quite inebriated and not as suspicious of Peter's disguise as he might otherwise be. The success of this ruse emboldens Peter, and he boasts of having repeated the trick on many occasions. Despite the risks of impersonating officers, it seems he is hardly ever recognised. It may be that he chooses his moments well, but it's clear that his ability to slip into the skin of a character is unusually convincing. He is later to claim that the *Goon Show's* dissolute Major Bloodnok was born of these late-night escapades.

On one occasion, the prank does backfire: Bill Sutton, a Gang Show veteran on an inspection tour of South East Asia Command, recalls that 'there was a party in some officers' mess and Peter … appeared in the middle of the party in the bloody [Group Captain] uniform. He was quite good until he got drunk and gave the game away. The commanding officer took umbrage and the whole Gang Show unit was put on a *fizzer* [a disciplinary charge].'[21] Sutton has to smooth things over with pleadings about artistic temperament.

Great efforts are made to ensure that, although they are thousands of miles from Britain, and maybe even quite a long way from the nearest town, RAF personnel are able to enjoy a traditional Christmas dinner. Where possible, chickens, ducks and occasionally even piglets are acquired in the autumn, for the express purpose of providing a taste of home. The record books contain lots of detail about this important subject, and there's a whimsical

An improvised bamboo-type stage: this one is at Silchar.

exchange of memos from the base at Cox's Bazaar with the catering section about what might be on the menu, and the preparations that are needed:

The type of poultry [should] be first established; whether it is of land-based type, requiring wired-in dispersals or runways, or whether of coastal or web-footed type ... In the event of the latter being the case, it is suggested that some suitable person be directed to get quacking.

The reply comes back:

... an amphibious type is being provided with web-footed undercarriage. It is recommended that a small basha hangar with slipway into fresh water is made available, and whole area fenced. The hangar would require to be made secure against intruder sorties. For your information, this type works best on a 100 octane mixture, grain, barley, dried peas and beans.

In any case you are not getting any until shortly before Christmas.

So, despite the privations of the rest of the year, on 25 December the men sit down to a proper roast lunch, with all the usual accompaniments, even cranberry sauce and stuffing. It is a tradition in the British forces that officers wait on the lower ranks before having their own meal. There is 'high tea' later in the day too. One troubling matter is often that of the Christmas beer ration; despite its being requisitioned well in advance, it seems to be problematic to guarantee its arrival. But with the excellence of the food and the general party atmosphere, everyone makes the most of the chance to take a few hours off from their hard work and relax. Printed Christmas menus are often included in the ORBs; the RAF produced blank covers for general use. An example can be seen opposite, from no.383 Air Ministry Experimental Station at Imphal:

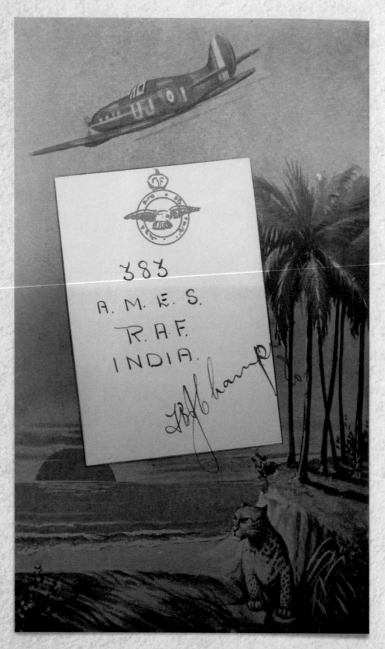

383

A. M. E. S.

R. A. F.

INDIA.

Cover of Christmas menu, 383 AMES, 1944.

January 1945

At the start of the New Year, George Taylor has written a letter to *The Stage*:

A Breath o' the Heather
A letter from A..C. George (G.F.X.) Taylor, who is with a R.A.F. gang show touring India. says he went out as Scots comic to try and bring " a breath o' the heather " to the lads out there frae Bonnie Scotland. The show already has covered over 12,000 miles and played at such extremes as the private theatre in the Maharajah's palace at Jodpur—a week at the New Empire, Calcutta—and then on to the jungle in Assam and Burma to play to the lads in the front areas and forward bases.

❋   ❋   ❋

GS10 are now in Comilla where they give three shows at the Town Hall over the New Year period. They then head south, towards the busy area of Chittagong. Allied Forces are progressing ahead of them in the same direction, gradually liberating Burma from the Japanese. Peter and three of his pals (opposite) find time for some war games of their own, though exactly who is being liberated here is not clear.

In Chittagong they perform in a Transportation Shed belonging to 92 ASP, where they are 'very much enjoyed by the Unit and numerous visitors'. The ORB is in no doubt about the value of such entertainments, which are:

> *… highly appreciated by all Service personnel and have contributed noticeably to an improvement in the morale of the men. The benefit accruing from these Shows cannot be too highly stressed.*

War games in Comilla: Peter with Ben Novak, Jimmy Patton and Harry Kane.

They then take over the cinema at 902 Wing HQ. Their three-night run here is probably rendered even more successful by the timely arrival of the month's beer ration. At Chiringa they have the luxury of an entire *basha* to themselves. This is just as well; some local workers on the base have been keeping a goat in their sleeping quarters, to protect it from predation by jackals. GS10 are the first entertainment at the new Station Cinema, playing to 901 Wing

. . . .

HQ, 177 and 211 squadrons over two nights, 15 and 16 January. The Cinema has been christened 'The Beaumont', an allusion to the Bristol Beaufighter aircraft deployed there, and a smart pun on Gaumont films.

Still following behind the front-line, GS10's next target is the cluster of bases around Cox's Bazaar. At Samader Bazar, a large *basha* has been built as an entertainment centre, some ten minutes' walk from the camp, and named 'The Casino'. It hasn't been very well used, 'a White Elephant' even, but the volunteer-run canteen next door to it has fared better. The ORB speculates 'maybe the European ladies who assist are an added attraction'. Who are these redoubtable women, one wonders? Maybe they are members of the Women's Auxiliary Service Burma (WASB), set up to organise mobile canteens in Burma Command.

The men of 149 Repair & Salvage Unit see GS10 at the Casino on 19 January. These jungle theatres are few and far between and can be quite rudimentary. At Dhoapalong, 131 R & SU reports: 'R.A.F. Gang Show No.10 appeared in the area and transport was arranged. Some 70 personnel went to the "Paddy Bird" Theatre*, a bamboo theatre built for the forward areas. The show was very good.'

The Imperial War Museum film

'*Two 1.5 ton Chevrolet lorries drive past camera with airmen on the running boards.*' Thus begins the IWM's summary of the main reel of their film. Maurice Arnold, Wally Sparks and Jimmy Patton are the men riding on the cab and Dudley Jones is directing operations on the ground; the others are pictured opposite, enjoying a ride inside. They are at Maunghnama airfield in Burma, and the date on the cameraman's chalk board is 26 January 1945. They are travelling to

---

* Paddy bird = a small indigenous heron, not to be confused with Patricia "Paddy" Burke, star of ENSA, who also had a theatre named after her, in Chittagong.

Akyab Island (now known as Sittwe), where they will become the first entertainment unit to play there following its recapture by Allied forces.

Their props and costumes are transported in large wicker hampers – these are the most durable containers, able to withstand considerable rough treatment on trains, planes and lorries. When they arrive we see them unpacking chairs and boxes onto the scrubby grass; Peter is clutching an enormous suitcase which bears his initials. Goodness knows how he has managed to smuggle this non-standard-issue item past the authorities. He is also seen in several shots keeping a tight hold of his enamel mug – they must be hard to replace if mislaid (and you're better off with your own germs than someone else's). There's a short section where they are gathering up their instruments – Peter is concerned about the strings on his banjolele and Maurice and Bill are tinkering with accordions. They all walk towards the camera, Peter giving a cheeky thumbs-up as he passes, and then we see him strolling along with Harry Kane, strumming and mugging while Harry fiddles. They seem oblivious to the fighter planes pottering around in the background.

In the back of a lorry at Maunghnama airfield, Burma.

Peter on banjolele with Harry Kane on violin.

The help of the local RAF Regiment is enlisted to rig up a makeshift stage. It's a bombed-out house with some drapes tied across the front, the ever-present Gang Show backdrop hung at the rear and posters with a sunflower design nailed below the footlights, proclaiming 'Gang Show – it's Bright and Breezy boys, it's the tops!' (Take a closer look, and there in the background behind the house is a small corrugated iron privy.) It is possible to match some of the filmed excerpts to the printed programmes from previous shows: 'Fish Queue' – four gossiping old ladies with their shopping bags and an outsized fish wrapped in paper; 'Merrie England', in which Patton has a sly fumble at the Queen's bosom; and 'In Town Tonight', where Peter, smartly dressed in blazer and slacks, "interviews" Dudley Jones, who is posing as the dimmest ERK [ground crewman] imaginable.

Ralph Reader has always been insistent that the "ladies" should be played by men in women's clothes, rather than by female impersonators: 'It must always be clear that it's a bloke in a dress.'[22] – that's the way to

. . . .

Peter with Dudley Jones: 'In Town Tonight'.

'It's the Tops'.

get the best laughs. One of the Gang Shows' most flamboyant alumni was Rex Jameson, whose stage persona, Mrs Shufflewick, seems to have permeated his everyday life, to the extent that his garrulousness, and his fondness for alcohol, reflected hers. His act would start with saucy lines such as 'If I'm not in bed by eleven, I'm going home.'

There is also a good deal of footage of the jazz quintet; if only the film had sound attached. Peter is singing along as he plays the drums and Maurice Arnold is making do with an accordion, pianos being rather harder to obtain in the forward areas. The audience is seated on the ground, on planks resting on oil drums, or standing at the back, laughing, clapping and joining in. They are not all servicemen – there are some local people too.

903 Wing HQ sums up: 'No. 10 R.A.F. Gang Show gave two shows on the 27/28 Jan. On the 28/Jan Lt. Gen. Christianson* [sic] was present at the show.'

February 1945

At this point in their story, GS10 turn back towards India. From Akyab their route will take them north via Calcutta, and thence to Agra. Bill Wilkie recalls this as a three-day journey by rail, arriving in Agra mid-afternoon on the third day and performing that evening. Though this sounds appalling, it would by now be quite normal for the Gang. The following day, 3 February, they move on to Salawas, on the outskirts of Jodhpur, where they play in the Station Cinema, with 'decided success', according to 355 Maintenance Unit. Next up is Bhopal for two days, then Nagpur – 'a wizard show'. They are heading back towards Bombay, and it seems that they return to the holding camp at Worli and give a show there, so they may think they are to be posted back to the UK. They also tread the boards of the RAF Theatre on Marine Drive (christened by GS4 back in

*Lt-Gen Philip Christison had been in command of the recent Allied landings at Akyab.

. . . .

December, just prior to their own repatriation). But the plan changes; they are not going home after all. Two days later, on 19 February, the fantastically-named School for Jungle Self-Preservation Training, at Mahableshwar (just outside Poona) announces:

> *The personnel of No.10 RAF Gang Show arrived from Poona. Our stage was quite adequate for their purpose, but the piano was found to be off tune.*

Quite possibly this was not at the top of the RAF's list of priorities. Nevertheless, the show, in the Sergeants' Mess the following day, is 'excellent and a really enjoyable evening … it is to be hoped that more of these shows are in India.' It is one of the first concert parties ever to visit the base – once again, GS10 boldly go to places which have previously been overlooked. Unfortunately, some of those stationed there have missed them, being on exercises in the jungle. On their return from a four-day survival training trek, 'they looked remarkably healthy when rid of dust and grime.'

Jimmy Patton, however, has been lucky. As one of the older members of the group, he is due for demob before the others, and he seems to have left GS10 and got himself onto a boat bound for Blighty. Interviewed in 1980 by a local newspaper in his home town of Rotherham, he tells of a letter he received from Peter dated 16 March 1945, in which plans for their post-war future are outlined. Peter has been Patton's right-hand man in some of the Gang Show sketches and it is proposed to continue this as a double act. 'I wrote a complete show for us … I was going to be Principal Comic, and Peter was going to be my feed.' – but Patton is already a civilian again, while Peter has a year or more to serve – and he is still in the Far East. Peter, however, has commissioned his mother to try to secure his early release. Ralph Reader's second-in-command is Flight Lieutenant Jack Cracknell, and he knows Peg Sellers well. Peg has tried everything she can think of – she has even given him a

GS 10 in Burma.
Jimmy Patton, second right.

tree for his garden in Sarratt, Hertfordshire. Peter writes to Patton 'Everything is definitely fixed with Reader … our contracts are just waiting for us to sign them.' But it comes to nothing, for Patton is unable to wait. He joins a show titled *Spivs & Drones*, and sets off on the variety circuit, but not without regrets: '[Peter] was a terrific performer, a joy to work with. We could see all the potential, for a great talent was there.'[23]

The chance is lost. Peter is on his way to Ceylon.

March 1945

If GS10 are disappointed at not going home, their next destination might have been specially chosen to lift their spirits. Ceylon is a delightful place, with a pleasant climate and beautiful scenery. They arrive in Vavuniya to find a more relaxed atmosphere and a large population of RAF personnel. They play in the station cinema there, and then in the NAAFI at Ratmalana, to a detachment of 292 squadron. From Minneriya, where 160 squadron find them 'first class entertainment', they head for the hills, to Radella, for the second of their periods of leave. 'After giving a show for about 140 personnel, all services, [they] remained on for a week's leave.' It is a verdant place, with spectacular views, and the proprietors of the tea plantations extend a warm welcome to their RAF visitors. Dudley Jones describes being persuaded, as usual, to perform unofficially in a little church hall: they are at such an altitude that, half way through the show, a cloud passes through the open sides of the building, enveloping all present, clearing seconds later so that they can continue.

26 March finds them in the capital, Colombo. Here, the RAF have requisitioned a girls' convent school and turned it into a theatre. The building still exists, in a shady site just off Maitland Crescent, having reverted to its original purpose as St. Bridget's. *Airflow*, the magazine of the RAF in Ceylon, rates GS10 highly, and gives some details of their activities thus far:

> *the first variety show to play to British troops stationed in Akyab … two evening performances were given to audiences over a thousand strong, and during a period of forty-seven days they presented forty-two shows in the forward areas.*[24]

This is an astonishing figure, since it must only cover the period between 10 December 1944 and 28 January 1945. They are back in Ratmalana on the following day and then they move on to the far south of the island, to a place Bill Wilkie describes as 'like a South Sea island with lagoons and palms, and beautiful beaches, the nicest place I have ever been to'[25]. This is Koggala, where GS10's arrival has been eagerly anticipated, despite the disruptive effect it has on the efforts of the station's own concert party. The ORB notes that 'the Concert Party is progressing well, and hoped to put on its show … at the end of March. Some difficulty is being experienced in arranging dates to fit in with the forthcoming visit of No.10 Gang Show.' Marjorie Smith, a WAAF on the station, gives a first-hand account of her own feelings about the Gang Show. She has has been working hard at a dance routine, and has made her own elegant, billowing skirt from old mosquito netting.

> *We were all rather annoyed when we were told by the entertainments officer that we'd have to stop our rehearsals as one of Ralph Reader's*

Gang Shows was visiting the station … they would want the stage, the dressing rooms and all the facilities.

Out of curiosity, Marjorie and some of her friends go to watch this bunch of 'Boy Scouts' in rehearsal: 'what an eye-opener – they really were terrific!' She is particularly impressed by the young drummer – 'I've never heard anyone play with the same skill.' She and Peter become friends, enjoying each other's company and the good things that Koggala has to offer. She remembers them eating fresh pineapples on the beach: 'sheer joy … the local Singhalese boys would fetch them for us for a few coins', and discussing their plans for life back in Britain after the war. Peter tells her of his ambitions to become a serious actor. Marjorie is in no doubt that he has the talent to achieve his goal. 'He would make us laugh until tears rolled down our faces with his impressions … his self-assurance and style … were nothing short of pure professionalism.'[26]

Gang Show no. 10 at Koggala. Sellers at rear.

Standing: Jones, WAAF, Osborne, Marjorie Smith, Taylor, WAAF; Sitting: Novak, Wilkie, WAAF, Kane.

Sunderland flying boat at Koggala.

The show is a success, running for three nights. The writer of the Entertainments report in the month's ORB, however, is in the minority: 'It seems a pity that so much of the comedy was slightly risqué.' This is a surprise, given Reader's efforts to keep the shows clean. Perhaps, after seven months presenting the same material, GS10 have started to embellish their show somewhat. They could hardly be blamed for deciding to freshen things up a bit.

April 1945

The war in Europe is coming to an end, and GS10, who have now been away for over eight months, are most definitely on their way home. Nine months seems to have been the average length of a tour. However, they still have a busy time ahead. Their route back towards Bombay takes them from Ceylon to South India; after visiting the station at Golden Rock – 'I don't think anybody in their right minds could have watched them with a straight face' says the station magazine *The Gremlin Times* – they are found on the western coast, at Willingdon Island, a station in the Cochin area. This is inconvenient: 'Entertainments were provided during the month by No.10 R.A.F. Gang Show and an E.N.S.A. Show. Unfortunately, their visits coincided, but local arrangements were made not to actually clash.' The ENSA show, *Sunrays*, plays first, followed by GS10 on 12 April.

At Arkonam, GS10 are erroneously described by 139 Repair & Salvage Unit as No.10 R.A.F. ROAD SHOW – but no matter; they are voted 'the best show that has visited this unit'. The Maintenance, Repair & Salvage units were among the forgotten heroes of the air war in the East. With improvised, rudimentary facilities, they were tasked with keeping the machines flying, in conditions way beyond those for which they were designed – extremes of heat, dust everywhere, and torrential rain being only some of the problems they faced. Often they had to dig out planes which had become bogged down in the monsoon mud; occasionally they were called on to repair an aircraft in which a mule had been transported, and it had kicked through the skin of the fuselage, in a panic, on leaving the ground.

No.2 Staging Post, at Gannavaram, are definitely impressed. The show is 'most welcome after a lapse of about 8 months.' At St Thomas' Mount, a beautifully hand-written ORB calls them 'excellent', the most popular of three visiting companies during the month: 'the Service Flavour of [the show] obviously appealed very strongly to the audience.' The unremitting schedule continues at Cholavaram ('admirable' and 'very well received') and Redhills Lake. At Avadi Camp, close to the centre of Madras, 337 Maintenance Unit has some shrewd critical observations to make. 'No.10 R.A.F. Gang Show … performed to a large and enthusiastic audience. During the same week ENSA [put on] "LET'S HAVE A PARTY". The appeal in this case was provided rather by the presence of the strong feminine element in the cast than by their artistic ability.' It seems that there is, indeed, 'nothing like a dame'.

The Gang Shows seem to have been generally more popular with audiences than some of the ENSA productions on the circuit. ENSA's standards were certainly more variable, as were the reviews they received in the ORBs. A friendly rivalry comes across in the records, and it's clear that the RAF took great pride in their own endeavours.

Among the ENSA groups touring the sub-continent during this period is Waldini & his Gypsy Band. The name crops up again and again in the ORBs, and though their itinerary doesn't coincide directly with GS10, they may well have encountered Peter on their parallel trajectories. Waldini's tour covers equally vast distances, and his accordionist, Elaine Parsons, is said to have worn out fourteen instruments.

GS10 next head north up the coast to Vizagapatam, 'thoroughly enjoyed by all', including some visitors from 8045 Experimental Station (these are radar installations, operating under strict secrecy, hence the non-committal unit name). And at their final stop this month, in Secunderabad for two nights, 'They were given a great ovation, and the men really did enjoy the show'.

GS10 are now on the final leg of their Indian odyssey. For all the difficulties posed by travel, climate and conditions – '28,000 miles in every known means of transport except a bullock cart' according to Dudley Jones[27] – this must have been the most exciting year of many of the men's lives. An intoxicating, exotic combination of spectacular cities and landscapes, a very different culture and the camaraderie of the unit will be things they will never forget. The last word might be a reminder from the ORB of a unit stationed on the Indian Ocean that the RAF must still uphold standards of Britishness, despite all that has gone on:

A large supply of … swimming trunks was obtained from Station Welfare, so there is no excuse now for swimming in the nude.[28]

. . . .

Chapter 4

BACK TO BLIGHTY

May–July 1945

O n 8 May, it is VE Day, and RAF personnel in India are celebrating. There is a party atmosphere at the Base Reception Depot in Worli with a full programme of entertainments, including 'an excellent dance … on the roof of No.2 SSQ [Station Sick Quarters] for ex-P.O.W's, the cost being borne by RAF Welfare funds.' Local expatriate European ladies are inviting servicemen to join them for a few home comforts: 'Mrs. Guildford entertained 4 airmen to dinner [and] Mrs. Bollings provided tea and swim to 4 airmen at the Willingdon Club'. GS10, awaiting news of their departure from India, are onsite and are co-opted to assist with the festivities. 'No.10 Gang Show provided a small cabaret.' No doubt this includes a set or two from the Jive Boys. Despite their imminent repatriation, 227 Group lists GS10 as touring stations in the group during the month of May. But the return to Britain, a tantalising prospect for so long, has finally become reality.

It seems that they sail on the same ship that brought them to India, the SS *Mooltan*. It's the same journey, of course, in reverse: leaving Bombay on 3 June via Suez, Port Said and Gibraltar, reaching the UK at Falmouth on 25 June. However, the ship continues on to Clyde before returning to Gravesend, where they are finally disembarked on 2 July. It is not uncommon for fully-loaded troopships to be delayed in processing, which must be incredibly frustrating for the men on board.

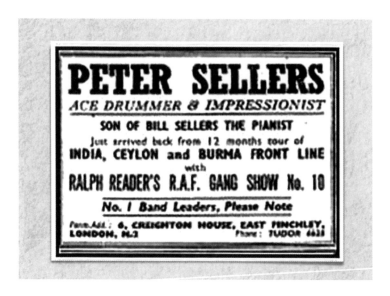

Advertisement in *The Stage*, 28 June 1945.

However, Peter's mother Peg isn't letting the grass grow under anyone's feet. On 28 June the above advertisement appears in *The Stage*.

There's something rather touching about Peg's faith in her son: 'No.1 Band Leaders, Please Note'! But it seems an odd thing to do, since he is far from being demobbed. However, there must be a degree of uncertainty about what will happen now that the war is all but over, and Britain is being overrun by returning troops. Happily, the first stage of re-adjustment is to take a short period of home leave. And GS10 isn't breaking up just yet – they are shortly to be despatched to a new frontier: the Isle of Wight.

> FOR ONE NIGHT ONLY.
> Special Appearance of
> **RALPH READER'S**
> **No. 10 GANG SHOW**
> at the **Town Hall, Ventnor,**
> on **Sunday August 19th, 1945.**
> TWO Performances, 6 and 8 p.m.
> Admission (at the Door):
> 3/6, 2/6, 1/6.
> **Don't miss it.**

Listing from the *Isle of Wight County Press*, 18 August 1945.

August 1945

RAF records in post-war Europe are much more matter-of-fact and less full of interesting detail than those from India and Burma. So, it is at this point that the trail of GS10 goes, if not cold, at least luke-warm. But we know from Bill Wilkie that the team are to spend a fortnight on the island in the Solent. To get there they probably travel from Portsmouth, Peter's birthplace and where, as a small boy, he enjoyed "conducting" the musicians on the bandstand at Southsea. The local press, in the form of the *Ventnor Mercury*, is excited about the forthcoming show:

> *It is always a treat to see a Ralph Reader Gang Show, and on Sunday next Ventnor is to enjoy a special performance of the No.10 Unit. These boys have just returned from a 50,000 mile tour of Burma, India and Ceylon, where they have been so great an asset and so greatly appreciated by our own gallant 14th Army.*

It details the cast, 'a star-spangled one', notably Peter Sellars [sic] 'whose impressions are not only accurate, but of stellar entertainment' and Maurice Arnold: 'We all wonder how Maurice can play those beautiful classics … for the BBC and still swing it so effectively in this show with the R.A.F. No.I Jive Band, which Ventnor people have already taken to their hearts.' The old pier in Ventnor is still extant in 1945, overlooked by the splendid Art Deco-style Winter Gardens theatre, half way up the zig-zag road that leads into the town. Perhaps the Jive Band has been informally entertaining holidaymakers as they begin to return to normality in this pleasant place, the southernmost part of the island, with predominantly fine weather in summer, and nothing but the English Channel between it and France. The finale of their stay will be, 'for one night only', two shows in the Ventnor Town Hall, on Sunday 19 August, at 6pm and 8pm. It is such a success that they are 'pressed to give a repeat performance on the following Tuesday, and again [play] to absolute capacity'. The *Isle of Wight County Press* adds 'Except for buses, it is not often that there are queues outside the hall, as on these occasions.'[29] Peter has impressed as usual with his accurate skit on *ITMA*. This must be all the more hilarious in the context of the national sense of relief at the outbreak of peace.

While all this has been going on, Graham Stark's GS4 has followed its Tour of the Far East by travelling to newly-liberated Europe: first Belgium and then Germany, where they come face-to-face with the reality of the atrocities which have taken place. Stark meets two starving children in Celle; he is shocked to see the numbers tattooed on their arms. On their return to the UK in August 1945, the show is dissolved and Stark is sent to Abingdon to run GS9, which has been in Italy and North Africa. This brings him together with Aircraftman Tony Hancock, and they are soon on the road again, on a visit to Gibraltar and the Azores. Others in this show include the actors Tony Melody, Robert Moreton and John Beaver. It seems that they spend the remainder of the year entertaining at bases in the UK and Europe. They make an extended

Gang Show no.9 (ii) at West Raynham, March 1946. Graham Stark (standing, in stripes), Tony Melody (front, second from left), Tony Hancock (centre, looking down), Robert Moreton (in deerstalker hat), John Beaver (far right, in hat and scarf).

stop at West Raynham in Essex in March 1946, where besides giving their show, they challenge the local WAAFs to a comic football match (the women trounce them, six goals to nil). There is a real sense that the RAF doesn't know what to do with these men, whilst they are waiting to be released from the service.

September 1945

In the cast roster from the *Ventnor Mercury*, the tenth named member of GS10 is compère Bill Adams, who has been with a show in the Middle East. After Patton's departure in February, they are of course a man short. It's not clear when Adams has joined – it may even have been in India. But this replacement is not a sign that GS10 will continue in its current form. All the returning shows are to be broken up and re-constituted according to how much time their members have already served and how long remains before their discharge. Meanwhile, Ralph Reader is about to be demobbed himself. His last production before returning to civilian life is to be a colossal 'Pageant of Victory' at the Royal Albert Hall, in aid of RAF charities and sponsored by the *Daily Telegraph*. Reader's expertise at staging events in this venue dates back to his pre-war Scout shows, some on an extremely large scale. This one is called *Per Ardua ad Astra*.

Rehearsals take place at a disused USAAF airfield known as Willingale, in Chipping Ongar, Essex. It's an ambitious programme involving set-pieces tracing the history of the Royal Air Force from its origins as the Royal Flying Corps. Gang Show staff back from tours and awaiting their new orders are roped in to help, as are hundreds of serving airmen and women. Sgt Margaret Diplock, who is based in Cornwall, is detailed to bring half-a-dozen fellow WAAFs to Essex. She tells a researcher from the Imperial War Museum that on arrival, they find GS10 already there, including Peter. 'He was the drummer … he took out any lovely girl he could find … he took out one of my girls, Molly Kingsley.' She describes him as 'great fun, an extraordinary character', and notes that Reader kept a close eye on him: 'We went out to celebrate Peter's birthday [8 September] and Ralph actually sent some transport to bring us back!' Shrewdly, she thinks this might be more for the girls 'protection than Peter's, pre-empting possible mischief. She doesn't remember him for his act, but 'he was a very good drummer.'[30]

There are lots of familiar names here: Bill Sutton and George Cameron from the Gang Show establishment, narrator Sgt Richard Attenborough, and the conductor Norman del Mar. Actress Martita Hunt is to appear with Peter in the 1960 film *Mr Topaze*. It is while working on the Pageant that Bill Adams meets, and is eventually married to, Babs Williams, a member of one of the WAAF Gang Shows which Reader has set up towards the end of the war, and the author of a book on the subject, *Halt! Who Goes There?*.

Another WAAF, Biddy Edwards, remembers being asked to volunteer – 'You, you and you.'[31] The accommodation at Willingale is filthy and they have to make it habitable themselves. When they have done so, they embellish the redundant RAF signage on the base, changing it to 'READER'S AIR FORCE'. After about three weeks' rehearsal they head for London where they stay in overcrowded Salvation Army Hostels during the production. A 'cast of thousands' – 2,500 according to the *Daily Telegraph* – combine in spectacular tableaux, displays of marching and music. One striking scene depicts a Sunderland flying boat searching for the crew of a ditched aircraft – a spotlight eventually illuminates the tiny dinghy, almost

ONDON DAY BY DAY

ST night's Pageant, sponsored y THE DAILY TELEGRAPH, was a nal triumph for its producer. Ldr. Ralph Reader. The whole' nsibility of the production from beginning has fallen on his ders and the magnificent way ich he rose to the opportunity estified to by several members e programme.

e layman can hardly realise the nt of organisation which goes e making of a great spectacle is kind.

Sqdn. Ldr. Reader, however, s been something more than hnical triumph. He has been the R.A.F. since the beginning e war and the arrangements he show were, for him, a labour re.

word is also due to the fine of Sqdn. Ldr. Alan Melville, throughout was perfectly in athy with a great theme.

he Royal Box

Commodore Strang Graham, irector of Air Force Welfare, is f the those Scots who keeps his gs to himself. He must, how- have been extraordinarily y at the Albert Hall last night. has always had a special for the badly wounded in his ce, particularly the badly d. If was some of these latter under his ægis occupied the Box at the R.A.F. Pageant. rs and other ranks—all were inder treatment.

er the Pageant they were taken by specially arranged transport e hospitals from which they in the late afternoon.

hopes their enjoyment was lete. The rest of the audience nly considered it a privilege they had been able to come.

Sqdn. Ldr. Ralph Reader
A Personal Triumph

Programme

Per Ardua ad Astra

A Pageant of the Royal Air Force

Script by Squadron Leader Alan Melville
Production by Squadron Leader RALPH READER, M.B.E.
Associate Producer : Warrant Officer W. A. Sutton

Stage Director :
L.A.C. Albert Locke

Costumes :
Warrant Officer George Cameron

The Central Band of the Royal Air Force
and
The Royal Air Force Symphony Orchestra
By permission of the Air Council

Massed Choirs of Units of Technical Training Command
By permission of the Air Officer Commanding-in-Chief
and
The London Choir School, Bexley
conducted by
Wing Commander R. P. O'Donnell, M.V.O.
(Organising Director of Music, Royal Air Force)

The Royal Air Force Central Band Dance Orchestra
By permission of the Air Council
Conducted by Sergeant J. Miller

Organist : Arnold Greir, F.R.C.O.
Music selected and arranged by Flying Officer John Hollingsworth
and Sergeant Leighton Lucas

Additional orchestral arrangements by L.A.C. Norman Del Mar
and L.A.C. Leonard Isaacs

Narrators - - James McKechnie By permission of Sydney Box Productions Ltd.
Lionel Gamlin

Henry Oscar
F./L. David King-Wood
Wally Patch

MARTITA HUNT
Sgt. Richard Attenborough
F./O. Bill McLurg

and

VIOLET LORAINE

(7)

Programme from *Pageant of Victory*, 'Per Ardua ad Astra'.

. . . .

swamped by mountainous seas. Dudley Jones has a speaking part and others present from GS10 include Wally Sparks, Maurice Arnold and George Taylor. There's no indication as to what Peter does in the production; he may simply be involved in the chorus and crowd scenes. The show runs for two nights, 19 and 20 September, and is attended by, among others, RAF casualties who are specially brought in from hospitals and seated in the Royal Box. Reviews (in the *Daily Telegraph* of course) proclaim it a personal triumph for Reader.

Autumn 1945

The Pageant over, Peter is to be found in the Gang Show office at no.15 Cadogan Gardens, in Knightsbridge, shuffling paper and keeping his ears open for any opportunities that might come his way. As he explains to a newcomer who arrives fresh from General Duties, being in London enables him to keep tabs on the current variety scene and hopefully make contacts that will be useful when he is finally demobbed. The new arrival is Cecil Buckland, ex-ENSA and starting his National Service. He will eventually become a popular TV personality in his native Scotland, under the name Glen Michael. He recalls Peter at this time as being slightly tubby, with lots of bushy hair. Presumably he is back living with his parents in Finchley and being fed to within an inch of his life. Also working in the office is Frank Thornton-Ball, who, minus the Ball, will later achieve comedy immortality as Captain Peacock in the 1970s sitcom *Are You Being Served?*

Buckland is sent to an outlying base at Chessington in Surrey to join up with a show which then plays at RAF stations all over the South of England. Peter will not be in the office for much longer either. A new version of GS10 is to convene in Gloucestershire to work up a programme which they will take on tour in France. His time in a desk job has been mercifully short. An incurable performer, he must be delighted to be liberated again and off on the next stage of his Gang Show adventures.

Chapter 5:

A NEW SHOW
FOR EUROPE

Peter, Les Osborne, Bill Wilkie and Wally Sparks join Sergeants Harry Herring and Clifford Henry, singer Freddie Beer, now calling himself Brent, and pianist Larry Doughty from the former GS6 (veterans of North Africa and the Far East) in a group which also includes actors Don Collin and Cyril Wright, George White (a trumpet player from Stanley Black's orchestra) and a Gang Show debutant, David Lodge. It is the latter's book, *Up the Ladder to Obscurity*, which gives us almost all the information we have about this new chapter in the story of Peter Sellers and the Gang Shows.

Peter is now twenty years old and embarking on his second tour of duty. He has his campaign medals – the Burma Star, War Medal and Defence Medal – and he is no longer the baby of the Gang. In David Lodge he finds a like-minded older brother figure, or a chaperone, according to Peg, but not always a very reliable one, and it is soon apparent that he has not lost his talent for getting into trouble. He doesn't get on well with Freddie Brent at first and needs Lodge's help to stand up to his bullying. Then, as they set off for France on 20 November after their warm-up performances, somehow Bill Wilkie's accordion gets left behind at the Air Ministry and there is a panic about catching the boat train – Bill has overslept and Peter has to wake him. In Paris they are billetted at the Magasin Dufayel where the beds are infested with bugs. It is as bad as the forests of

Portrait of Peter from the time of his tour of duty in Europe.

Burma. A swift decision is made to find alternative lodgings, but the rooms they choose, in the nearby Pigalle district, are not exclusive to them – they are also occupied by some professional ladies, who seem only too keen to make their acquaintance. David Lodge apparently decides that's a more acceptable risk than being eaten alive, and with perhaps a pang of regret they barricade the door with a wardrobe before settling down for the night. Bill, who has caught a later train with Cyril Wright, is certainly surprised when he arrives in the small hours and is directed to the Gang's new quarters.

They travel south from Paris in a convoy of trucks and motorised caravans, learning as they go that certain commodities which are easy for them to lay their hands on, via the Service Clubs, are of great value on the black market in France. Peter is a born hustler – his childhood spent dealing "antiques" with Peg has taught him to be wily and shameless – and he gleefully assumes the role of spiv-in-chief. They trade chocolate and cigarettes for cash, as well as selling blankets and warm clothing given to them at the stations they visit. It is, in David Lodge's words, 'a glorious orgy of free enterprise'[32]. They nearly get into real trouble when local bootleggers ask to purchase some of their petrol rations – on returning to the caravans after the show, they find the bandits in the process of robbing them of the rest of their fuel. Freddie Brent chases them away, helped by Peter, whose banjo case is mistaken for a machine gun in the darkness (yes, really!).

They wend their way via Lyons, where their show is made more interesting by the fact that they have been treated to quantities of special local "apple juice" before going on stage, then to Avignon and Toulon, eventually arriving on the French Riviera, where they visit Bandol and Marseilles. In Marseilles they again try their luck at selling petrol, concealed under their RAF overcoats in large jerry-cans, cartoon-comedy fashion, but are thwarted by finding that their chosen rendezvous, a bar called *La Toupée*, is full of officers and they are lucky to make good their escape unnoticed.

At Istres, they find themselves in the middle of a work-to-rule by disillusioned staff at the staging post there. And at Bandol, Lodge has a lucky escape when he almost wanders off the edge of a cliff after a few too many glasses of wine. Eventually they arrive in Cannes, whose glamour is only slightly diminished by the effects of the war.

Their accommodation, at the Hotel Montana, is splendid and the weather is fine. It is a dream posting for them and they are keen to make the most of their leisure time. They decide to take a ride on a motor boat. Lodge is the first to try a swim in the alluringly blue waters of the Mediterranean. Appearances can be deceptive – it is, after all, December – and he is out of the freezing water almost as fast as he goes in.

On the way back to Paris, they play to one of their smallest audiences – just twenty men – at a tiny radar station in the foothills of the Pyrenees, and in Bordeaux, on 19 December, they entertain civilians as well as the RAF in the Town Hall at Merignac – probably a real treat for those recently liberated. They are in Paris in time for Christmas. ENSA has taken over the Marigny Theatre for its varied programme of entertainments, and GS10 is booked for a week's run, starting on Christmas Eve. Lodge remembers Peter and the 'Gang Show Jive Boys', now comprising George White on trumpet and Larry Doughty on piano, with Bill Wilkie and Les Osborne, spontaneously playing 'When the Saints Go Marching In' on the back of their truck as they drive along the Champs-Elysées towards the theatre. The show, '100 Minutes of High Speed Variety', includes a pantomime, *Jack and the Beanstalk*. Their accommodation in Paris is opposite the Opéra Comique, and they use the profits from their 'free enterprise' to reward themselves with a private box, and champagne, for a performance of *La Bohème*.

In Dieppe, Lodge is treated to one of Peter's impersonations. He is on his way to the fish market and laden with cans of bully beef to barter, when he encounters an unusual sight, a Sikh officer with full beard and turban, who interrogates him about the contents of his pack.

The Sikh officer is of course Peter, but he cannot keep up the ruse; he gets the giggles – a lifelong weakness when amongst friends – and cheekily asks the enraged Lodge to be sure to get him a nice Dover sole.

There is an impression that they are largely unsupervised at this stage of their careers; there is far more freedom than was possible in the Far East, mainly because they are never in any real danger now that the war is over. Peter is getting bolder, on and off stage; the fearlessness and disregard for authority that will be remarked on throughout his life is now fully in evidence, though at the age of twenty, it probably still seems no more than youthful cockiness.

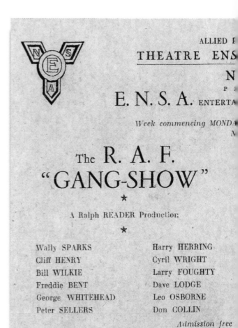

ALLIED F
THEATRE ENS
N
P
E. N. S. A. ENTERTA

Week commencing MOND

The R. A. F.
"GANG-SHOW"
★

A Ralph READER Production

★

Wally SPARKS	Harry HERRING
Cliff HENRY	Cyril WRIGHT
Bill WILKIE	Larry FOUGHTY
Freddie BENT	Dave LODGE
George WHITEHEAD	Leo OSBORNE
Peter SELLERS	Don COLLIN

Admission free

GENERAL MANAGER
E.N.S.A. I

Programme from the Marigny Theatre, Christmas 1945.

January–April 1946

In the New Year of 1946, GS10 mark 2 are to be found in Germany, where the RAF has a large presence as part of the Allied forces of occupation. It is an exceptionally cold winter. Aircraft are frequently grounded because of heavy snow and even road travel is challenging. The show's arrival in Detmold is eagerly anticipated. Change is afoot; Wally Sparks has left the party and there is a new name on the cast list, Barry Lowe. And Peter has received a promotion, to AC1 (Aircraftman, 1st Class).

MENTS

NY - PARIS

ALLIED FORCES

th 1945 *(including 25th)*

THE GANG-SHOW JIVE BOYS
JACK and the BEAMSTALK
etc.

100 MINUTES OF
HIGH-SPEED VARIETY

Sunday December 30th 1945 : CELEBRITY CONCERT

SPECIAL GALA

Geneviève CHAUVIERE, contralto
Jean DOYEN, pianist
Henry MERCKEL, violinist
Accompanist : André COLLARD

Next week : " WALK-UP ! WALK-UP ! " Gay Circus Revue

All Silverware in use at the Marigny Theatre supplied by CHRISTOFLE

os *in uniform*

EDWARD STIRLING
ERMONT

The *Air Division Times*, a newspaper produced by the RAF in Detmold, announces GS10's imminent appearance at the 'Casino' Theatre 'direct from Uxbridge where it has been in rehearsal', but it's not clear when, or if, they have in fact been back to the UK. The RAF has taken over the former Detmold Landestheater as an entertainment venue, and it presents a varied programme: military and swing bands, stage plays, tea dances and even an opera, *Hansel and Gretel*. GS10 performs on two successive nights, 20 and 21 January, and there is a half-page review in the paper the following week. We learn that Freddie Brent has been unexpectedly recalled to England, so Bill Wilkie has to deputise in the vocal numbers, 'so well that the song might have been designed exclusively for him'. Cliff Henry and Cyril Wright do comic impressions and Don Collin plays virtuoso musical saw (a now-forgotten skill from the days of vaudeville). The writer thinks that No.10 'maintains the high standard set by previous shows' but that it feels different – 'the emphasis has shifted ... we have one eye on civvy street now.' The pantomime is 'glorious': Cyril Wright is Principal Boy, Harry Herring is the Good Fairy ('slightly moth-eaten') and Barry Lowe is the Princess. But the changes in personnel have not affected the show's polish. 'Only those who have had actual experience of stage work can possibly know the amount of hard work necessary to achieve such seemingly easy team-work'.

The highlight of the programme was undoubtedly the band consisting of George White, trumpet, Peter Sellers, drums, Les Osborne, sax and clarinet, Bill Wilkie, piano-accordion and Larry Doughty on the piano. Here was hot music dished up just as the audience wanted it and they showed their approval in no uncertain manner. Worthy of mention in this act was a trumpet solo by George White and some energetic drumming by Peter Sellers.[33]

There's also a column in the following week's *Air Division Times* headed 'The Mystery of No.10'. It's worth reproducing this for its informative detail about the way each Gang Show evolved over time.

THE MYSTERY OF No. 10

There seems to have been a certain amount of controversy over No. 10 Gang Show. Prior to its arrival, [one of us] maintained that he had seen it … somewhere or other and asserted it "wasn't 'arf good". Agreeing with the latter part of this statement, we feel we must enlighten him on the former.

The present No. 10 Gang Show is a combination of the former No. 6 and No. 10 and the show you saw last week is called "No. 10" merely because that number became vacant.

We have, for our authority, Sgt. Herring who, with Sgt. Henry, is in charge of the party. He tells us that the show left England as recently as Nov. 20 and toured the southern part of France. The performance here is their second in Germany. All in all, members of the company have played in 28 different countries, including India, Burma and Iceland.

We don't know about Iceland but we can testify to the fact that touring Germany on the back of a three-tonner in this weather is no piece of cake either!

This seems to contradict the suggestion that they have been back to the UK to rehearse. But 'RAF Light Entertainment' is certainly based at Uxbridge in this post-war period. The RAF Theatre/Cinema is one of the few period structures extant there. It is a listed building and has been incorporated into the current redevelopment of the site, with plans for its use as a museum.

David Lodge relates that Peter's impersonations of senior officers have become a regular thing during their travels in Germany. He reasons that they rarely stay anywhere long enough for anyone to become suspicious. As Peter later remembers: 'In the early morning we would be off again to the next stop. No-one knew or cared who the young officer in the bar was or where he had gone.'[34] Lodge is often drawn into the game, to his great discomfiture: he is sure that it will all end in tears. He can't believe that Peter isn't recognised as the same person who has earlier been performing on the stage – especially when he joins in with the local band in the Officers' Mess. Peter's most audacious stunt comes at Gütersloh, where he decides to dress as a Flight Lieutenant and inspect the lower ranks. There has recently been heavy rain causing flooding in the camp and morale is low. He lends a sympathetic ear to their complaints about food and accommodation, promising that he and his wing-man (Lodge) will convey all that they have heard back to the powers that be. He argues that this way, the men will feel that someone cares about them. Lodge, squirming with embarrassment, finally drags Peter away, under protest. Peter is addicted to danger and somehow they always stay one step ahead of the court-martial.

In Bückeburg, they encounter something completely new – an all-female Gang Show. Ralph Reader's big idea in 1944–5 was to establish these units, to meet an undoubted demand among the yet-to-be-demobbed men still stationed away from home. Babs Adams, in her book *Halt! Who Goes There?* describes her experiences in the WAAF shows, with contributions from colleagues including Elsa Crawshaw and Pat Oates. Pat has passed through RAF Abingdon in the summer of 1945, where she meets Graham Stark and Tony Hancock rehearsing for their trip to Gibraltar. Later she auditions to Jack Healy and Norrie Paramor at a Gang Show office in Ashley Gardens near Victoria Station. Then she is off to Germany to join up with WAAF Gang Show no.2, close on the heels of our No.10. *Air Division Times* has heard about them: 'the tame sleuths of the Casino are endeavouring to trace [their] whereabouts in order to arrange [an] appearance here.'[35]

The photograph shows traces of snow falling, but it isn't dampening the enthusiasm of the group. Peter is clearly doing his best to keep up morale and Elsa Crawshaw (to his left) is fully entering into the spirit of it all. Pat Oates describes the occasion: 'My opening night with the girls was hilarious ... we were greeted by thunderous applause from a packed theatre. From a box at the side came wolf whistles and we glanced up to see who was making the noise. It was No.10 RAF Gang Show in walrus moustaches. What a night!'[36]

Gang Show no. 10 (ii) and members of WAAF Gang Show, outside the "Brau House" in Bückeburg.

The Gang (WAAF style) - Sellers second from the right at back row; Elsa second from right in the front row

Gang Show no. 10 (ii) with the WAAFs in Germany. David Lodge at rear, left.
He grew a moustache, specifically to avoid being cast as a woman.

At Bad Godesburg, GS10 are accommodated at the Rheinhotel Dreesen, a splendid place with a notorious past: it had been a favourite of Adolf Hitler who kept an exclusive suite of rooms there and it was the venue for a meeting between him and British Prime Minister Neville Chamberlain in September 1938, in advance of the signing of the 'Munich Agreement' ('Peace for our time!'). As things are becoming more relaxed in Germany, a dance is held at the hotel, during which Peter and David Lodge have paired off with a couple of WAAFs from a nearby station. It is late when they offer to walk the girls down the long wooded drive to the main road, to catch their bus back to base. The moonlight creates a suitable ambience, and at the crossroads they decide to progress things a little further, huddling down behind a derelict tank while waiting for the bus to arrive. They are rudely interrupted by two officers of the law; one a British Military Policeman, and the other a German civilian. Having ascertained that the lads are not 'fraternising' with local women, they send the girls safely on their way, honour intact. It is then that they warn our two would-be seducers against wandering about at night. It is the first time they have heard of the 'Werewolves', though the idea

Gang Show no.10 (ii) in Blankenese, a suburb of Hamburg. Seated: Lowe, Wright, Collin, White, Doughty, Wilkie. And a dog. Standing right: Henry.

seems appropriate to the Gothic atmosphere. The policemen explain that there is a resistance movement of German forces still active in the shadows, calling themselves *Werwölfe* and using guerilla tactics against Allied servicemen who stray off the beaten track. This seems to have been more of a rumour than reality, but it certainly has the desired effect upon Peter and his useless chaperone – they bolt back to the hotel, their suave self-confidence in tatters. Such incidents undoubtedly influence future *Goon Show* humour, much of which is inspired by the comic/disastrous potential of service life.

Peter is behind the camera for this picture (*above*) showing some of GS10 (ii) in the garden of the *Sagebiels Fährhaus*, a regular

The Sagebiels Fährhaus, used as an informal HQ for British forces in the Hamburg area.

meeting and eating place for Allied forces. This find offers early evidence of his lifelong obsession with, and skill in, photography. He later became friendly with Lord Snowdon, and his pictures were occasionally published in *Vogue* and other society magazines.

After the liberation of Germany, the British Forces' Broadcasting Service took over the Hamburg Musikhalle (now the Laeiszhalle) for their headquarters. This had previously been the premises of Radio Hamburg, from where the traitor William Joyce, known as "Lord Haw-Haw", regularly broadcast propaganda ('Germany Calling!') intended to demoralise the British.

While performing at the Garrison Theatre in Hamburg, Peter is seen by LAC John Jacobs, who runs variety shows for the British Forces Network (he is the brother of radio presenter David Jacobs). He finds Peter's act 'very funny'[37] and invites him along to the Musikhalle to make what is probably his first ever solo radio broadcast. While there is no detail as to what this involves, it could be a segment in the programme *Service Varieties*, described in the BFN listings as a music hall programme by artists in uniform, with

Peter broadcasting in uniform.

guest artists from the civilian variety stage. The BFBS's historian, Alan Grace, tells us that Jacobs also crosses paths here with an army comedian named Harry Secombe, but is less impressed.

Summer–Autumn 1946

In contrast to their hectic schedule in India and Burma, this tour of Europe seems almost leisurely. They are still in Germany at Easter; on 29 and 30 April they give shows in Lüneburg. David Lodge is demobbed when the show reaches Schleswig-Holstein, in the far north, leaving Peter, who has over a year's service remaining, feeling somewhat lost. But it is not long before the rest of GS10 is back in England, probably in May. Peter's travels are now at an end and he returns to clerical work to see out his time in the RAF. He resumes living with his parents and obtains a large and shiny American car – the first of many such vehicles he is to own; this one is probably a gift from Peg, who must be delighted to have her boy home at last. It is on a visit to the Air Ministry at Houghton House that he meets Graham Stark, soon to be demobbed and killing time in London in the meantime. Stark is living at a servicemen's club near Victoria Station, where the clientele is so dubious that it's advisable to put the legs of your bed into your shoes before retiring, lest they be stolen. They quickly become friends and Peter arranges lodgings for Stark with a neighbour in High Road, East Finchley. They spend a considerable amount of time at the Nuffield Centre in Wardour Street where there is a regular supply of attractive servicewomen at the evening dances. It is at this time that Peter encounters Tony Hancock, who is also working in administration for the Gang Shows. Both are temporarily employed in the Light Entertainment stores at Uxbridge, where they enjoy camping it up in the guise of two old theatricals, "Mr de Sellers" and "Mr le Hancock", dishing out costumes and pretending to be 'in the know' with all the showbiz gossip. Hancock is depressed; 'How long are we going to be stuck here?' he is frequently heard to moan, in a vein that we can recognise as characteristic of his later radio and television alter ego.[38] Peter, meanwhile, likes to tease the WAAFs who pass by the stores, with an alarming turn as Dr Jekyll/Mr Hyde.

In June, Hancock has been promoted to Sergeant, as Gang Show no.9 morphs into yet another configuration to prepare for a tour to Japan. But at the last minute he is unable to travel, through illness. He remains in London and eventually produces a new version of Gang Show no.4. In this party are Peter Reagan – the father of the actress Carol Drinkwater; Barry Martin – still active in film and television until his death in 2017; and Rex "Shuff" Jameson. As in the case of Cecil Buckland, there are now young men being called up for National Service, to add to those still awaiting discharge; one such recruit to GS4 is the jazz pianist Stan Tracey, who meets Peter at Cadogan Gardens and describes him, somewhat dismissively, as the 'office boy'. In Tracey's opinion, the pool of talent is running dry; it is becoming more difficult to keep up standards, but Hancock manages to 'whip something together'[39]. Hancock himself is demobbed at the beginning of November, and GS4 continues in the Middle East without him, appearing in Cairo in December.

In September 1946, Peter receives simultaneous promotions, first to Leading Aircraftman and then to Acting Corporal (paid). This does not bring instant rewards, however. He is still a desk-jockey, occupying his time with what we'd now call networking, helping out anywhere he can, trying to make contacts. The Gang Shows are, incredibly, still going on – a group of demobbed veterans from the

Peter with a car, and his corporal's stripes, 1946.

. . . .

earliest shows is touring UK theatres throughout 1946, promoted by the impresario Tom Arnold, and overseen by Reader; Dick Emery and Cardew Robinson are the stars. ENSA has been wound up, and other services' concert parties have merged into a new organisation, the "Central Pool of Artists". Yet the Air Ministry is still sending groups overseas, with more men on even longer tours. Why are they needed, more than a year after the war has ended?

In fact, the RAF retains a presence in many areas where they have been stationed during the conflict, and given the backlog of men serving out their time in the force, the continued existence of the Gang Shows is perhaps as much for the benefit of the entertainers as the entertained.

Back at the mother-ship, however, Peter doesn't have enough to do. As with other tour-expired members of the organisation, it seems that the RAF turns a blind eye if he isn't in the office all the time. As early as December 1945, George Taylor has made an announcement in *The Stage*, giving his contact address as 'RAF Variety Unit, Air Ministry, 160 Ashley Gardens SW1' and stating that he is 'available Sunday concerts only until demobbed in January.' So actively seeking work may even be officially sanctioned. Wally Stott, later to become Music Director on *The Goon Show*, remembers bumping into Peter, still in his RAF uniform, waiting with other unemployed musicians in a West End hangout where band vacancies are advertised. However the niceties are dealt with, Peter is almost certainly taking paid dates before he leaves the service. Besides gigs as a drummer, there are tales of him performing at fairgrounds and amusement parks, a tough apprenticeship at the most junior level of the variety business. His parents are friends with the Parkin family, who own a holiday camp in Jersey, and it's likely that he is employed there during this period. He even dates Hilda Parkin for a while. That the RAF allows him considerable licence despite not being demobbed probably indicates that they just don't have the resources to keep tabs on his whereabouts.

. . . .

'The Ship's Concert' from Wings.

1947

The doldrums extend into the spring of 1947. Now Ralph Reader comes to the rescue again. As Ralph Reader Ltd, he is cooking up another spectacular show, to be called *Wings*, which will tour the UK, ostensibly as a recruiting tool for the Air Council. To produce it, No. 30 Pageant Unit is formed at RAF Uxbridge in March 'for rehearsals for eventual tour of the country'. Tony Hancock finds himself drafted in, now as a civilian, as are the other ex-Gang Show members that Reader calls up – Reg Dixon, Bill Sutton, and Norrie Paramor. After five weeks they all decamp to RAF Warton in Lancashire for the final stages of preparation. The show opens at the Blackpool Opera House on 28 April. Leslie Melville, who grew up in the town and has spent his life as a magician and entertainer there, is fourteen at the time. He remembers seeing the show, and says 'in [it] were the then unknown Peter Sellers [and] Tony Hancock.'[40] Peter isn't on the bill of this production, but photographs collected by Hancock archivist Malcolm Chapman show that there is a huge cast of extras, described as 'Serving Airmen and Airwomen'. It is easy to assume that Peter is probably one of these; he may have stepped in at some point to cover for an indisposed colleague. There is someone who might be him visible in one of the pictures (circled opposite). Hancock is the Dame at the front of the stage.

Wings tours for over twenty weeks, ending almost back where it began, in Morecambe. Peter's involvement is likely to have been sporadic, as he doesn't have a speaking part, and in any case, by the time it returns to Lancashire in September, he has finally been demobilised. He resumes his civilian life on 7 July 1947. He is twenty-one years old.

Chapter 6:

CODA

Peter's eventual discharge from the RAF must feel like the final act of a pitch-black comedy, blurting him out into a world saturated with unemployed ex-servicemen and entertainers, many of whom fall into both categories. Notwithstanding an encouraging note from Jack Cracknell on his release certificate – 'The above-named is strongly recommended for any work with entertainment' – he is now a tiny fish in an enormous pond. And yet, his career is at last in his own hands. Ten years later, in 1957, when Cracknell invites him back to open a Scouts' Summer Fete in Hertfordshire, Peter's speech includes a description of how Cracknell offered him the chance to remain in the RAF for another two years. 'I care not what happeneth to you, Jack,' declaimed the young scallywag, 'but I am demobilised.'[41]

Royal Air Forces Association and reunions

Peter seems to have been ambivalent about mentioning the Gang Show in his publicity post-war; he may think it suggests amateurism. Nevertheless, he retains a strong connection with the RAF. He joins the Highgate Branch of the Royal Air Forces Association and on 12 September 1948 he is on the bill of a Festival Of Reunion staged at the Royal Albert Hall in aid of the charity.

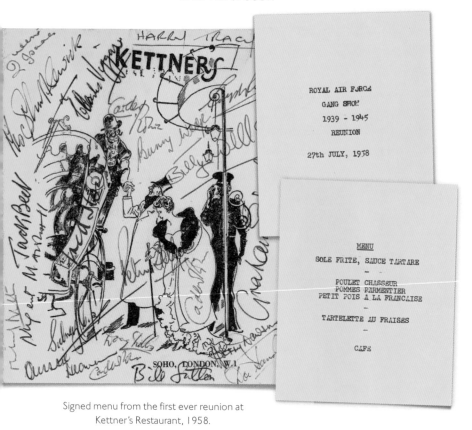

ROYAL AIR FORCE
GANG SHOW
1939 - 1945
REUNION

27th JULY, 1958

MENU
SOLE FRITE, SAUCE TARTARE
—
POULET CHASSEUR
POMMES PARMENTIER
PETIT POIS A LA FRANCAISE
—
TARTELETTE AU FRAISES
—
CAFE

Signed menu from the first ever reunion at
Kettner's Restaurant, 1958.

Artistes who appear include Vera Lynn, Richard Attenborough and another Forces' Sweetheart, singer Anne Shelton. The producer? – Ralph Reader of course. The RAFA journal, *Air Mail*, reports that 'Peter Sellers, up-and-coming impressionist … was an outstanding success.'[42] Later, when living at Chipperfield Manor in Hertfordshire, he is invited to become the first President of the Abbots Langley Branch of RAFA, formed in 1959. Their history records that 'he attended one function … a dance.'[43]

But his main contribution to the ongoing Gang Show story is to initiate what will become an annual reunion. His efforts to bring his old comrades together begin with an advertisement in *The Stage* in April 1958: 'Members of R.A.F. Gang Show Units who are interested in the possibility of a Reunion are invited to send their names and permanent addresses to PETER SELLERS, 37, Panton Street, S.W.1.' This idea is enthusiastically received. Elsa Crawshaw has remained friendly with many of the men from the shows, including 'Pete' (Sellers) and 'Hank' (Hancock), meeting up at the Nuffield Centre while they all await their demob (though Hancock won't dance, because he is sure he's too clumsy). Peter writes and recruits her to bring the WAAFs along: 'Dave, Cardew, Graham, we're getting the lads together, can you get the girls together, for we must not lose each other!' The first reunion takes place at Kettners Restaurant in Soho on 27 July 1958; the following year it is at the Dorchester Hotel. On this occasion Peter, who clearly has a soft spot for Elsa, pins an orchid onto her dress. The warmth is mutual: she describes him as 'a good friend and a true gentleman.'[44]

The Royal Air Force Gang Show Association is formed as an umbrella organisation, and they continue meeting into the 21st century, though inevitably the numbers have dwindled. In 2001, Elsa and her remaining comrades rendezvous at St Clement Danes, the RAF church in the Strand, where the Gang Shows are commemorated by a stone memorial in the south pavement, and then at the London School of Economics in nearby Houghton Street for a meal. There is a plaque celebrating the Association in the Old Theatre there.

And so at this point, we can let other biographers take up the story of how Peter struggles to be noticed ('Peter Sellers, Drums & Impressions, Bang On!'), appearing in regional variety programmes in front of unimpressed audiences, until he visits an agent, George Knapman, who advises him to cut the drumming from his act and manages to secure him a six-week stint in 'Revudeville' at the legendary Windmill Theatre in March 1948 ('among the nudes' he would say, with a mournful expression, if asked what it was like).

....

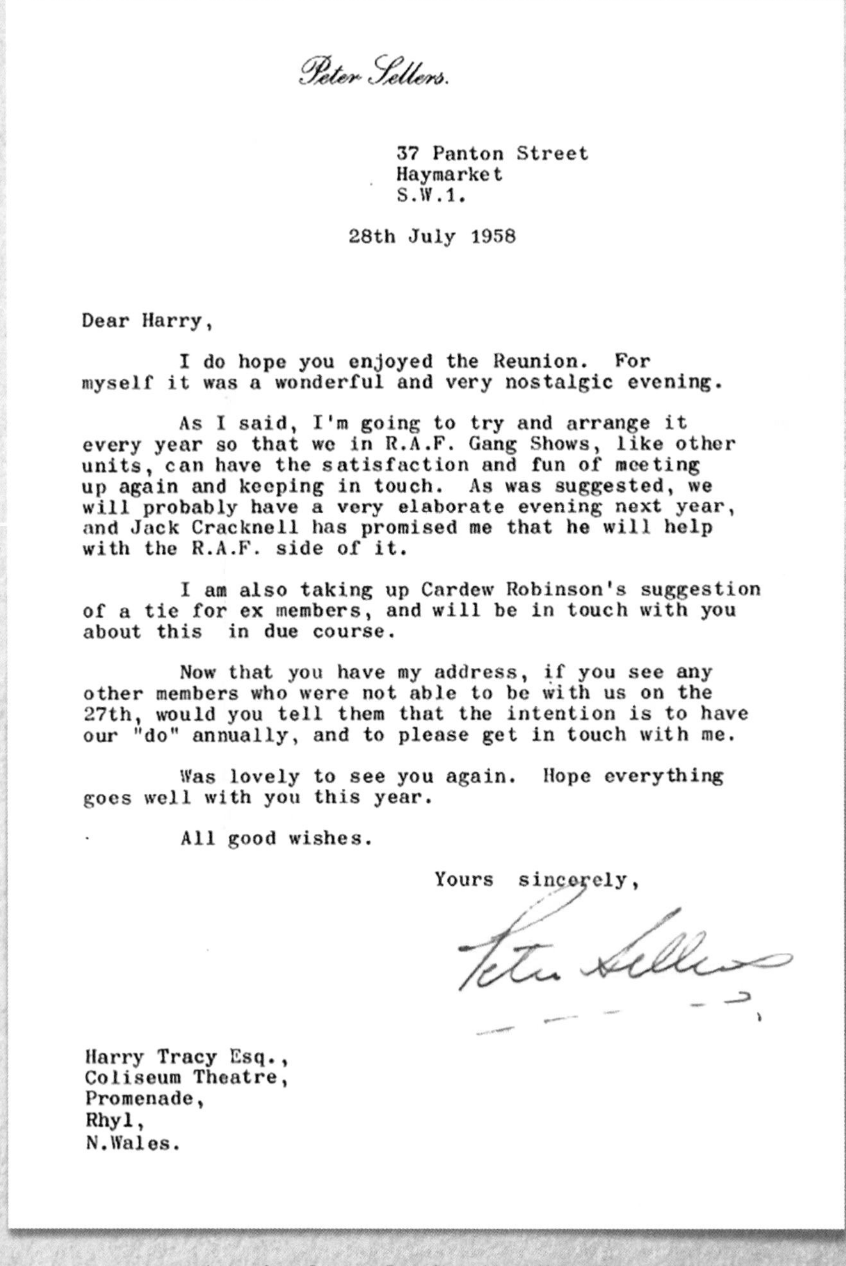

Peter Sellers.

37 Panton Street
Haymarket
S.W.1.

28th July 1958

Dear Harry,

I do hope you enjoyed the Reunion. For myself it was a wonderful and very nostalgic evening.

As I said, I'm going to try and arrange it every year so that we in R.A.F. Gang Shows, like other units, can have the satisfaction and fun of meeting up again and keeping in touch. As was suggested, we will probably have a very elaborate evening next year, and Jack Cracknell has promised me that he will help with the R.A.F. side of it.

I am also taking up Cardew Robinson's suggestion of a tie for ex members, and will be in touch with you about this in due course.

Now that you have my address, if you see any other members who were not able to be with us on the 27th, would you tell them that the intention is to have our "do" annually, and to please get in touch with me.

Was lovely to see you again. Hope everything goes well with you this year.

All good wishes.

Yours sincerely,

Peter Sellers

Harry Tracy Esq.,
Coliseum Theatre,
Promenade,
Rhyl,
N.Wales.

Letter from Peter to Gang Show legend Harry Tracy.

Added by director Vivian van Damm to the honours board outside, 'Stars of Today Who Started Their Careers in This Theatre', his name is surrounded by others redolent of the high days of mid-twentieth-century light entertainment – Jimmy Edwards, Harry Secombe, Alfred Marks, Michael Bentine, Bill Kerr, Arthur English, Tony Hancock and so on to Bruce Forsyth.

One of Peter's early publicity shots, from a 1949 magazine.
The Montague Lyon agency was based in Jermyn Street,
which might account for the dapperness of his appearance.
Gallons of Brylcreem must have been required?

From left to right: Cardew Robinson, Ralph Reader,
Dudley Jones, Peter, David Lodge, 1962.

1962

On 9 September 1962, the RAFA and the RAF Gang Shows
Association combine to stage a Battle of Britain Week Gala in
London, at the Victoria Palace Theatre, in aid of RAF charities.
A large cast of Gang Show alumni take part, among them Peter
Sellers. He is characteristically generous with his time on these
occasions (he also regularly turns up at special events at the
Windmill Theatre) despite being, by this time, a bona fide star with
films such as Stanley Kubrick's *Lolita*, *The Millionairess* and *I'm All
Right Jack* on his CV. Others appearing include Reg Dixon, Ron
Moody, Alfred Marks, and the ubiquitous Rex "Shuff" Jameson. It is
all orchestrated by Reader, of course. He is seen above getting some
help with a pesky bow tie from Cardew Robinson, Dudley Jones,
Peter, and David Lodge.

Peter's act consists of some drumming, accompanying four pianists, one of whom is Larry Doughty; a couple of impressions, and then a '60-second quick change into what Florence Nightingale looked like in 1873', emerging wearing a Viking helmet and a red beard – having 'forgotten what she looked like'[45]. Sellers completists will note the similarity to his turn as Queen Victoria when appearing as a guest on *The Muppet Show* in 1978.

This is the last occasion on which Peter is involved in such an event, but it shows that he has an enduring bond with those who shared his wartime experiences. The friends he made in the Gang Shows are to remain his closest throughout his life. He goes to the reunions, when his schedule allows, and he maintains contact with Jack Cracknell, Bill Wilkie, Harry Herring, and others. The page below from the 1962 Gala programme is signed for Harry Tracy, perhaps the most splendid 'man in a dress' from the shows.

Above: Signed page of 1962 Gala Programme. **Top right:** Harry Tracy, at work.

Researching the history of his wartime service has helped to build up a picture of how the young Peter Sellers developed his performing styles, techniques and attitudes in response to the conditions and audiences which he experienced. Servicemen were notoriously hard to please and they were expert at heckling. It would take very little time to learn what worked and what needed to be edited or excised. In particular it seems that, far from their being amateurs, there was a high degree of professionalism in the Gang Shows, and Peter translated this into an obsessive perfectionism which in his later career would often antagonize his colleagues. He was generally thought confident and fearless, treating tough audiences with unflinching scorn, and he was not afraid of hard work. He was also fascinated by India and its people, noting their calm and cheerful demeanour and an acceptance of occasionally chaotic circumstances with forbearance and charm. He told the film critic Dilys Powell 'I liked the Indians ... their placidness, their good temper'[46]. This first-hand experience, though clearly gained from a Western, pre-Independence, perspective, seems to have been a largely positive influence. While his portrayals of Indian characters are likely to be seen as politically incorrect today, they are undoubtedly intended as sympathetic, even heroic, for example Dr Kabir in *The Millionairess*, who refuses to place any value on material wealth. In later life Sellers was also to take an interest in Eastern faiths, becoming friendly with Ravi Shankar and, through the record producer George Martin, George Harrison and his fellow Beatles.

Service humour was often mildly subversive, rather than openly insubordinate, giving as it did a legitimate outlet for the frustrations and absurdities of life in the ranks. There's a subtlety and astringency to much of Sellers' best work, which is quite different from the broad humour of some pre- and post-war entertainment. His great talent was for assuming a character completely, and given good quality material, making that character totally believable. In the fast-paced, two-hour Gang Shows, this needed to be done in an instant, so that a sketch would be immediately involving and the audience's attention be held. Whereas many of the next generation of comedians had their training in university drama societies such as the Cambridge Footlights, he had the Gang Shows. The experience he gained during these three-and-a-half years made him much more mature as a performer than others of a similar age. He also learned to improvise, with a jazz musician's instinct for timing, and developing ideas.

But most importantly, he learned about himself; how he could be anyone, or no-one, with equal skill, transforming himself in a split second, or slipping into anonymity. He was able to answer the telephone in a hundred different voices so that even his closest friends could not recognise him. In the early years of his career, this appears to have been a kind of exhilarating game (as well as a useful alibi), but as he became more well-known, the unreality of life in the media spotlight, and the dwindling influence of his own personality, may have contributed to some of the difficulties he experienced. However, he continued to produce fine work, culminating in the film many consider among his best, *Being There*, in the year before his death.

It has often been said that one of the great strengths of the British serviceman is his ability to maintain a sense of humour, even in the most difficult circumstances. This was certainly true during the Second World War, which, surprisingly, proved to be the crucible that forged the careers of some of the best-loved entertainers of the twentieth century, among them, Peter Sellers, The Man Who Was Bluebottle.

Sellers was always happy to be asked to play the drums, as is evident from many of his subsequent appearances on TV talk shows.

'INSIST ON SELLERS'?

Throughout his adult life, one of Sellers' favourite practical jokes was to post spoof notices in newspapers and magazines such as *The Stage*, to fool his fellow Goons and other friends.

The day after GS10 finished their run of shows at the New Empire Theatre, Calcutta, in December 1944, an advertisement appeared in the *Calcutta Statesman* newspaper (right). A pair of eyes gazes out from the page, with text as follows:

TRY SELLERS' LOTUS HONEY
for all EYE TROUBLES even Cataract, make sure World Wide reputed and tested. At all Chemists. Literature free. Frank Ross & Co. Calcutta. Kemp & Co. Ltd, Delhi. Insist on "SELLERS."

Advertisement from the *Calcutta Statesman*, 8 December 1944.

It is of course impossible to prove, and the chemist in Calcutta (just round the corner from the theatre!) is genuine, as can be seen from the advertisement adjacent. But it is tempting to think that this could be the first example of such a prank by Sellers and his pals. The chemist would be mystified by requests for a non-existent product - the jokers meanwhile having made their escape. Could it be that Peter's flair for misdirection and mischief is alive and well, with more puzzles such as this one waiting to be discovered? Maybe he is still having the last laugh.

APPENDIX I:

Peter Sellers: RAF career timeline

1943

19 December	Call-up: sent home on reserve 20 December

1944

13 January	To no.2 Recruits Centre, Cardington
8 April	Seconded to Air Ministry Unit at Houghton House
	Joins Gang Show no.10: 3 weeks' rehearsal in London
30 May	First show at Houghton House, then run-outs in the UK
7 July	To no.5 Personnel Despatch Centre, Blackpool
11 July	Show in Blackpool at the B.C.S. Jubilee Theatre
17–18 July	ACSEA posting – SS *Mooltan* sails from Liverpool for India (carrying 4118 troops, as part of convoy KMF33)
14 August	SS *Mooltan* arrives Bombay
16 August	Assigned to the command of ACSEA HQ, New Delhi (main HQ in India: all the Gang Shows are listed as based there)
21–31 August	On tour in Bombay area (227 Group)
25 August	RAF Santa Cruz/Sion: first show in India
September and October	Northwest India and North India, Delhi (from where their show is broadcast)

. . . .

13, 14 October	Chittar Palace performances, under the auspices of RAF Jodhpur
November	West Bengal
5 November	Calcutta: invited to dinner at no.2 Aircrew House
1–7 December	New Empire Theatre, Calcutta: daily shows at 10.30am
December	Recording for Columbia Records in Calcutta; Band Gala "8 'til late"
	Touring 221 & 224 Groups: Northeast India, Assam and towards the Burmese border

1945

January	Bengal, Assam, Burma
26–28 January	Akyab (Burma) – filmed by RAF film unit
February	North & Central India
17 February	Bombay (Marine Drive Camp theatre)
March	Ceylon (James Patton is demobbed and leaves India?)
16 March	Peter writes a letter to Patton about post-war plans
April	South India
May	Touring 227 Group (HQ: Bombay)
8 May	VE Day – cabaret at BRD Worli
6 June	Departs Bombay on SS *Mooltan*
25 June	SS *Mooltan* arrives back in UK
19, 21 August	Ventnor Town Hall, Isle of Wight
September	RAF Willingale (Chipping Ongar, Essex) – Pageant rehearsals
19–20 September	RAF 'Pageant of Victory' at Royal Albert Hall
Autumn 1945	Gang Show office, 15 Cadogan Gardens, London
	To Gloucester for re-formed Gang Show no.10
20 November	To France: Avignon – Marseilles – Lyon – Istres – Bandol – Toulon – Marseilles again – Cannes – Pyrenees – Bordeaux

19 December	Promoted to Aircraftman – 1st Class
24–30 December	Paris – Marigny Theatre – daily performances for ENSA

1946

January	Germany: Bad Godesberg, Bückeburg
20, 21 January	Detmold
8 February	Gütersloh
	Broadcasts on BFN at Musikhalle, Hamburg
29, 30 April	Lüneburg
May	Meets Graham Stark in Houghton Street
June/July	Office work at Cadogan Gardens – meets Stan Tracey
13 September	Promoted to Leading Aircraftman, then Acting Corporal (paid)

1947

April	"Wings" at Blackpool Opera House?
7 July	Demobbed at 101 Personnel Dispersal Centre, Warton, Lancs

APPENDIX II:

RAF Gang Shows in the Second World War

According to statistics collected by Richard Fawkes:

1939 November	1 show
1941 January	2 further shows
1942 November	3 further shows
1943 September	1 further show
1943 November	3 further shows
1944	3 further shows

WAAF SHOWS:

1944 June	No.1 unit
1944 December	No.2 unit

For the shows Ralph Reader wrote 163 original songs, 123 sketches, 71 production numbers and countless individual "gags".

In February 1944, the Air Ministry reported that the Gang Shows had already travelled in total 339,000 miles, each show averaging 15,000 miles per year.

Up to 31 May 1945, a total of 9,755 performances had been given.

Areas visited: Arabia, Belgium, Burma, Ceylon, Corsica, France, Germany, Gibraltar, Iceland, India, Iraq, Italy, Malta, 'Middle East', North Africa, Palestine, Persia, Syria, West Africa

Original show, France, November 1939 ("Ralph Reader & Ten Blokes from the Gang Show"), under the auspices of ENSA
Ralph Reader, Jack Beet, Norman Fellowes, Eric Christmas, Bill Sutton, George Cameron, Laurence Patrick, George Merridew, Bill Thorne

GSI (1940–)
Jack Healy, Bill Sutton, George Cameron, Bill Dickie, Murray Browne, Jack Beet, Eric Christmas

. . . .

GSI 1943 (from a programme at the Queensberry All Services Club in Soho)
Jack Healy, Fred Stone, Michael Moore, Charles Viggars, Ray Rowlands, Joe Smith, Arthur Tolcher, Len Snelling, Wally Sparks, the Tornado Twins (Frank & Fred Cox, later known as the Cox Twins)

GSI (France 1944, pictured below, with Ralph Reader, seated third from right)
Jack Healy, Ray Rowlands, Charles Viggars, Arthur Tolcher, John G Taylor, Danny Jarrett, Jerry Leslie, Len Snelling, Joe Smith, Al Bush, Dick Emery, Frank Cox, Fred Cox

GS2 (Blackpool 1942?)
Dudley Jones, Harry Tracy, Reg Dixon, Joe Baldwin, Cardew Robinson, George Cameron, Bill Dickie

GS3 (India 1945)
Dave McMurray, Rex Ramer, John Sands, Don Saunders, Jerry Green, Tom Harper, Dan Sprawling, Harry Rosenquit, Arthur Budd, Dan McIntosh, Bill Phillips, Cyril Eldridge

GS4 (North Africa, Italy, India, Burma, Ceylon 1944)
Sgt Bill Dickie, Graham Stark, EJ Bancroft, I (Sid) Cipin, Gordon FL Craig, JW Harvey, Leslie WQ Hatfield, JC Mitchell, T Pollard, Richard Walter

GS4(ii) (Middle East 1946–7)
Sgt Tony Hancock, Stan Tracey, Rex Jameson, Peter Reagan, Barry Martin, Wally Sheppard

GS5 (France 1944)
Cardew Robinson, Tony Davenport, Joe Black, Dick Carlton, Jim Stirling, Jock Wilson, Charlie Hickey, Rudi Mancini, Harold Honess

. . . .

GS6 (North Africa, India 1943–4)
Jack Beet, Reg Dixon, Terry Cole, Joe Gibbons, Stan Williscroft, Cliff Henry, Len Astor, Harry Herring, Larry Doughty (later, in India, Fred Beer/Brent, George Prescott)

GS7 (Wales 1944)
Sgt Dudley Jones, Len Lowe, Bill Lowe, Danny O'Dea, John Beaver

GS9 (North Africa, Italy 1944–5)
Fred Stone, Robert Moreton, Tony Melody, Joe Browne, Tony Hancock, Frank Bishop, John Beaver, Jimmy Baker, Sandy Land, Derek/Arthur Scott, George Gridneff

GS9(ii) (Gibraltar, Malta, UK 1945–6)
Sgt Graham Stark, Tony Hancock, Robert Moreton, Jack Fossett, Tony Melody, John Beaver, "Chippy" Carpenter, Leonard Kentish, David Kentish, Arthur Tolcher, Bert Blake

GS9 (iii) (Japan 1946)
Johnny Ladd, David Kentish, Leonard Kentish, Chippy Carpenter, Bert Blake

GS10 (India 1944–5)
Sgt Dudley Jones, Sgt Wally Sparks, James Patton Elliott, George Taylor, Norrie Paramor (then Maurice Arnold), Les Osborne, Bill Wilkie, Harry Whitney (then Ben Novak), Harry Kane, Peter Sellers (+ later Bill Adams)

GS10(ii) (France, Germany 1945–6)
Sgt Harry Herring, Sgt Cliff Henry, Wally Sparks, Larry Doughty, Don Collin, George White, David Lodge, Peter Sellers, Bill Wilkie, Freddie Brent (Beer), Cyril Wright (+ later Barry Lowe)

GS12 (Gibraltar, Italy, North Africa 1945)
Leon Dodd

GS13 (India 1945)
Conrad Vince, Vic Brooker

GS15 (Middle East 1946)
Jack Edwards, Miles Lee, Len Gamlin, Douglas Gordon, Tim Dormonde, Jerry Gosley, Terry Morgan, Len Fearnehough, Douglas Muscroft, John Hodge, Ralph Moat, Phil Rogers

Others who served, unit numbers not known:
Sonnie Allan/Leitch, Cecil Buckland, Bob Clanford, Jack Cliffe, Dougie Cunningham, Sonny Dawkes, Harry Dawson, Eric Delaney, Austin Evans, Charles Gray, Billy Harris, Frank Havenhand, Will Hay Jr, David Hughes, Ronnie Jordan, Albert Locke, Alfred Marks, Nugent Marshall, Syd Meads, Ron Moody, Stan Mortensen, Michael Northen, Frank Plummer, Rex Roper, Russell Rowe, Victor Seaforth, Jim Stirling, Bunny Wedge, Vic Weldon, Billy Wells, Harry Worth

(Further local shows were created on bases abroad, under the supervision of previous members no longer on active service. It is likely that some of the above men, e.g. Alfred Marks and Ron Moody, were involved in these shows, which were not officially numbered.)

. . . .

APPENDIX III:

RAF Gang Show no.10 in India, Ceylon and Burma, 1944–45

1944			Source (TNA)
Aug	14–16	Arrival in Bombay	
	21–31	*Touring 227 Group*	
	25	Santa Cruz/Sion (Bombay), 1st show in India	
Sep	5	Ambala	1 Sch AFTT
	14, 15	Risalpur (Nowshera)	144 R&SU
		Upper Topa	
	19	Peshawar inc. broadcast	141 OTU
	22–25	Samungli	21 C&M Party
	25–27	Quetta	7 SchTT/84 SQN
	29, 30	Drigh Road (Karachi)	320 MU
Oct	2	Drigh Road	
		Korangi Creek	
	9	Jiwani	45 SP
	13, 14	Jodhpur	319 MU
		Four days in *Delhi*, inc. broadcast	
		Palam (now Delhi Gandhi Airport)	353 SQN
	20, 21	Cawnpore	
	23, 24	Chakheri	
	25	Allahabad	308 MU
	27	Phaphamau	352 MU

Nov	2	Baigachi (with flies)	
	5	Dinner in Calcutta no. 2 Aircrew House	
	8	Chandipur (Balasore)	590 AMES
	10	Cuttack	
	12	Egra	248/543 AMES
	13	Khargpur	91 ASP
	14	Salbani	
	16	Digri	
	29/30	Dhubalia	23 APC/288 AMES
Dec	1–7	Calcutta, New Empire	
	11	Silchar	94 ASP (EP)
	13	Kumbhirgram	45 SQN
	15	Wangjing (nr Imphal)	98 ASP
	16	Tulihal	906 Wing HQ
	17	Tamu	907 Wing
	18, 19	Imphal (221 Group HQ)	194 SQN
	20	Kangla[tombi]	60 SQN/42 SQN
	21, 22	Palel	363 MU/909 wing
	30	Comilla	364 MU

1945

Jan	1, 2	Comilla	
	8	Chittagong	92 ASP
	11, 12, 13	Chittagong	902 Wing HQ
	15, 16	Chiringa	177/211 SQN
		Jumchar (Cox's Bazar)	2 FR / 138 SQN
	19	Mambur (Samader Bazar – Casino)	149 R&SU
	22	Dhoapalong	131 R&SU
	26–28	Akyab	903 Wing HQ
Feb	3	Agra	
	4	Salawas (nr Jodhpur)	355 MU
	5	to Bhopal	1 AGS

	11–13	Nagpur	315 MU/1301 Met
		BRD Worli	
	17	Bombay (Marine Drive Camp)	
	20	Mahableshwar (nr Poona)	Jungle training
March		*Trincomalee* (Ceylon)	10 FR
	9, 12	Vavuniya	
	10, 11	Ratmalana	292 SQN (det)
	14	Minneriya	160 SQN
	18	Radella – 1 show then a week off	7 Hill Depot
	26	Colombo (RAF Theatre)	
	27	Ratmalana	81 SQN
	29, 30	Koggala	
April	1	Koggala	
		Golden Rock (Trichinopoly)	2 CMU
	12	Cochin (Willingdon Island)	312 MU
	14	St Thomas Mount (Madras)	1302 Meteo
	16	Cholavaram	
	17	Redhills Lake	
	18	Avadi Camp (Madras)	337 MU
		Arkonam, Gannavaram	139 R&SU, 2 SP
	28	Vizagapatam	8045 AMES
	30	Secunderabad	2964 RAF Regt
May	1	Secunderabad	
	8	BRD Worli – VE Day cabaret	
		Touring 227 Group	
June	3	Departure from Bombay	

(Venues listed in italics report a visit "during the month", not giving the exact date. The SEAC newspaper, produced in Calcutta, wrote on 5 December 1944 that the total number of performances during GS10's tour would be in excess of 140.)

. . . .

APPENDIX IV:

WAAF Gang Shows 1944-6*

Irene Ansell, Iris Banks, Doreen Brown, Elsa Crawshaw, Irene Cutter, Melina Dingwall, Lorna Ellerbeck, Joan Gillingham, Peggy Gillingham, Joy Hiller, Dorothy Hobson, Kay Holder-Nesse, Amy Humphries, Queenie Isaacs, Jill Knight, Margaret Lawrence-Jones, Jennie McAndrew, Peggy McKinnon, Nina Maloney, Peggy Moore, Pat Oates, Micki Speake, Pam Tyler, Molly Watson, Babs Williams, Joan Wood, Micki Wright

*As listed by Babs Adams in her book *Halt! Who Goes There?*

APPENDIX V:

Abbreviations

AC1	Aircraftman, 1st class
AC2	Aircraftman, 2nd Class
ACSB	Aviation Candidates Selection Board
ACSEA	Air Command South East Asia
AGS	Air Gunners School
AMES	Air Ministry Experimental Station
AMU	Air Ministry Unit
APC	Armament Practice Camp
ASP / (EP)	Air Stores Park / (Equipment Park)
BFBS/BFN	British Forces Broadcasting Service/British Forces Network
BNR	Bengal Nagpur Railway
BOAC	British Overseas Airways Corporation
BRD	Base Reception Depot
C & M	Care & Maintenance party
CMU	Civil Maintenance Unit
DAFW	Department of Air Force Welfare
Det	Detachment
ENSA	Entertainments National Service Association
Erk	slang for a raw recruit; may be short for "Air Mechanic"
FR	Filter Room
IWM	Imperial War Museum, London
LAC	Leading Aircraftman

LSE	London School of Economics
Lt Gen	Lieutenant General
Met/meteo	Meteorological Flight
MU	Maintenance Unit
NAAFI	Navy, Army & Air Force Institute
ORB	Operations Record Book
OTU	Operational Training Unit
PDC	Personnel Despatch Centre/ Personnel Dispersal Centre
R & SU	Repair & Salvage Unit
RAFA	Royal Air Forces Association
RAF Regt	RAF Regiment
Sch AFTT/TT	School of [Air Force] Technical Training
SEAC	South East Asia Command
S/LDR	Squadron Leader
SP	Staging Post
SQN	Squadron
SSQ	Station Sick Quarters
TNA	The National Archives, Kew
USAAF	US Army Air Force
WAAF	Women's Auxiliary Air Force

(Place names in India and Burma have been spelled as they appear in the relevant ORBs.)

LIST OF SOURCES

Quotations from records at The National Archives

SS *Mooltan*	BT/389/21/85 (Merchant Shipping Movement Card)
Santa Cruz	AIR 28/679
Sion	AIR 29/143/2: No.4 Base Signals Depot
Ambala	AIR 29/749/1: No.1 School of Air Force Technical Training
Risalpur	AIR 29/808/4: 144 Repair & Salvage Unit
Samungli	AIR 29/821/10: 21 C&M Party – 'Dakota'
Quetta	AIR 29/750/1: No.7 School of Technical Training – 'a great success'
Drigh Road	AIR 29/1077/6: 320 Maintenance Unit
Korangi Creek	AIR 28/433
Jiwani	AIR 29/463/10: 45 Staging Post
Jodhpur	AIR 29/1078: 319 Maintenance Unit
Allahabad	AIR 29/1075/1: 308 Maintenance Unit
Phaphamau	AIR 29/1083/3: 352 Maintenance Unit
Baigachi	AIR 28/41
Egra	AIR 29/181/14: 543 Air Ministry Experimental Station
Khargpur	AIR 29/785: 91 Air Stores Park
Dhubalia	AIR 29/704/12: 25 Armament Practice Camp
Air Forces Welfare Bulletin	AIR 24/1423
Silchar	AIR 29/786/2: 94 Air Stores Park
Kumbhirgram	AIR 27/457/17: 45 SQN
62 SQN	AIR 27/584/15
Palel	AIR 26/500: 909 Wing HQ

. . . .

Cox's Bazaar	AIR 25/943: 224 Group – 'Ducks'
Chittagong	AIR 29/786/1: 92 Air Stores Park
Samader Bazar	AIR 29/165/3: No.2 Filter Room
Dhoapalong	AIR 29/806/9: 131 Repair & Salvage Unit
Akyab	AIR 26/494: 903 Wing HQ
Salawas	AIR 29/1083/5: 355 Maintenance Unit
Nagpur	AIR 29/864/2: 1301 Meteorological Flight
Mahab[a]leshwar	AIR 29/754/1: School of Jungle Self-Preservation Training
Minneriya	AIR 27/1066/5: 160 SQN
Radella	AIR 29/493/4: No.7 Hill Depot
Koggala	AIR 28/432
Willingdon Island/ Cochin	AIR 28/160
Arkonam	AIR 29/807/7: 139 Repair & Salvage Unit
Gannavaram	AIR 29/460/2: No.2 Staging Post
St Thomas' Mount	AIR 29/864/3: 1302 Meteorological Flight – 'excellent'
	AIR 28/679 – 'service flavour'
Cholavaram	AIR 28/143 – 'admirable'
	AIR 29/704/10: 21 Armament Practice Camp – 'very well received'
Avadi Camp	AIR 29/1081/9: 337 Maintenance Unit
Vizagapatam	AIR 29/192/4: 8045 Air Ministry Experimental Station
Secunderabad	AIR 29/137/5: 2964 SQN RAF Regiment
RAF Brown (Cocos Islands)	AIR 28/160: 129 Staging Post – 'swimming trunks'
BRD Worli	AIR 29/510
Uxbridge	AIR 28/1144

Books

Adams, Babs: *Halt! Who Goes There?*, Moorleys, 1994

Behan, Dominic: *Milligan (The Life and Times of Spike Milligan)*, Methuen, 1988

Draper, Alfred: *The Story of the Goons*, Severn House, 1977

Elliott, Paul & Barry: *Fifty years of To Me … To You*, The World's Fair Ltd., 2014

Evans, Peter: *The Mask Behind the Mask*, Severn House, 1981

Fawkes, Richard: *Fighting for a Laugh*, Macdonald & Janes, 1978

Fisher, John: *Tony Hancock*, Harper, 2008

Forbes, Bryan: *A Divided Life*, Heinemann, 1992

Franks, Norman: *Fighter Pilots over Burma*, Pen & Sword, 2013

Goodwin, Cliff: *When the Wind Changed: the Life & Death of Tony Hancock*, Century, 1999

Grace, Alan: *This is the British Forces' Network*, Sutton Publishing, 1996

Hancock, Freddie & Nathan, David: *Hancock*, HarperCollins, 1969

Hughes, John Graven: *The Greasepaint War*, New English Library, 1976

Lodge, David: *Up the Ladder to Obscurity*, Anchor Publications, 1986

Loveday, Jack: *RAF and Raj*, 2002

Michael, Glen: *Life's a Cavalcade*, Birlinn Ltd., 2008

Pertwee, Bill: *Stars in Battledress*, Hodder & Stoughton, 1992

Reader, Ralph: *Ralph Reader Remembers*, Bailey Bros. & Swinfen, 1974

Shapiro, Jill Millard: *Remembering Revudeville*, Obscuriosity Press, 2014

Shope, Bradley G: *American Popular Music in Britain's Raj*, Univ. of Rochester Press, 2016

Sikov, Ed: *Mr Strangelove*, Sidgwick & Jackson, 2002

Stark, Graham: *Remembering Peter Sellers*, Robson Books, 1990

Stark, Graham: *Stark Naked: an Autobiography*, Sanctuary Publishing, 2003

Walker, Alexander: *Peter Sellers, the Authorised Biography*, Weidenfeld & Nicholson, 1981

Online resources

BBC History: WW2 People's War
http://www.bbc.co.uk/history/ww2peopleswar/stories/50/a4360150.shtml – Jodhpur
http://www.bbc.co.uk/history/ww2peopleswar/stories/76/a4618776.shtml – Biddy Edwards

Box and Fiddle Archive: Bill Wilkie
https://boxandfiddlearchive.weebly.com/bill-wilkie-mbe.html

The Times newspaper: Bill Wilkie obituary
https://www.thetimes.co.uk/article/bill-wilkie-m3c690s3r

Airfields in Midnapore: Tony Donell's diary
http://www.midnapore.in/arifield/salboni-airfield-life-at-salboni.html

Imperial War Museum: RAF Gang Show in Akyab, Burma (film)
https://www.iwm.org.uk/collections/item/object/1060028825

Imperial War Museum: Margaret Diplock (audio interview)
https://www.iwm.org.uk/collections/item/object/80016272

Imperial War Museum: Fred Pentland-Firth (audio interview)
https://www.iwm.org.uk/collections/item/object/80026266

Imperial War Museum: Life in Air Command South East Asia (film)
https://www.iwm.org.uk/collections/item/object/1060038306
http://www.colonialfilm.org.uk/node/5430 (needs Internet Explorer browser)

SoundCloud: Maurice Arnold & his Jive Boys
https://soundcloud.com/tajmahalfoxtrot1/come-out-wherever-you-are-by
https://soundcloud.com/tajmahalfoxtrot1/doggin-around-by-maurice

London School of Economics
https://blogs.lse.ac.uk/lsehistory/2018/02/21/evacuation-to-cambridge/
https://blogs.lse.ac.uk/lsehistory/2017/11/10/gandhi/ (illustration of the Old Theatre)

P & O: The *Mooltan*
http://www.pandosnco.co.uk/mooltan.html

Graeme Fraser: RAF 159 Squadron & Dad's War
http://www.graemefraser.net/raf159squadron.html

Air of Authority – A History of RAF Organisation
http://www.rafweb.org/index.html

Stan Tracey
http://www.stantracey.com/biog.htm

London Gang Show Fellowship – Archive
http://lgsf.org.uk/archives/

Tony Hancock Appreciation Society
http://www.tonyhancock.org.uk/

Watford Observer: Sellers opening Scouts' Fete
http://www.watfordobserver.co.uk/news/10509539.display/

Watford Observer: Abbots Langley RAFA
http://www.watfordobserver.co.uk/news/4207366.Veterans__group_celebrates_50th_anniversary/

Our Oxhey: Jack "Flight" Cracknell obituary
http://www.ouroxhey.org.uk/wp-content/uploads/cms/Flight_A.pdf

Articles

Sunday Standard, Bombay: "Gang Show No.10 now in town" (from the column
   Calcutta Calling): Dec 3 1944

SEAC Newspaper, Calcutta: "RAF Gang Show is on its way": Dec 5 1944

The Stage: "RAF Gang Show comes to life again": Sept 13 1962
   "A Showbiz Dynasty"[Elliotts]: Dec 17 1981
   Various obituaries & advertising

My Weekly: "He Was Just One Of The Boys" [Marjorie Smith meets Peter Sellers in
   Ceylon]: June 6 1980

Rotherham Star: "It was nearly the Sellers and Jim show": August 9 1980

. . . .

NOTES

1. interviewed on *The Simon Dee Show* (LWT), 18 January 1970

2. told in Richard Fawkes: *Fighting for a Laugh*

3. told in Ralph Reader: *Ralph Reader Remembers*

4. told in Richard Fawkes: *Fighting for a Laugh*, as above

5. Programme for Gang Show no.10, New Empire Theatre, Calcutta, December 1944

6. *The Times*: Bill Wilkie obituary, 15 May 2017

7. Telegram from Richard Fawkes collection

8. Programme from New Empire, Calcutta, as above

9. *Box & Fiddle* Magazine archive: Bill Wilkie MBE, written by Norrie Williams

10. Dudley Jones, interviewed by Richard Fawkes for *Fighting for a Laugh*

11. *Box & Fiddle*, as above

12. Dudley Jones interview, as above

13. Ibid

14. Alexander Walker: *Peter Sellers*

15. Dudley Jones interview, as above

16. Ibid

17. Bradley G Shope: *American Music in Britain's Raj*

18. *Melody Maker*, 21 April 1945

19. quoted in Dominic Behan: *Milligan (The Life and Times of Spike Milligan)*

20. BBC Audio: *Parkinson meets the Goons*, 1973

21. quoted in John Graven Hughes, *The Greasepaint War*

. . . .

22. told in Bill Pertwee: *Stars in Battledress*

23. *Rotherham Star*, 9 August 1980

24. *Airflow* magazine (RAF Ceylon), April 1945

25. *Box & Fiddle*, as above

26. *My Weekly*, 6 June 1980

27. Dudley Jones interview, as above

28. TNA: AIR 28/160: 129 Staging Post, Operations Record Book

29. *Ventnor Mercury*, 17 & 24 August 1945, & *Isle of Wight County Press*,
    25 August 1945

30. IWM, Margaret Diplock audio interview (cat. no. 16830)

31. BBC *WW2 People's War*, Biddy Edwards: Life in the Women's Auxiliary Air Force

32. David Lodge: *Up the Ladder to Obscurity*

33. *Air Division Times* (Detmold), January 1946

34. quoted in Alfred Draper: *The Story of the Goons*

35. *Air Division Times*, as above

36. quoted in Babs Adams: *Halt! Who Goes There?*

37. Alan Grace: *This is the British Forces' Network*

38. Freddie Hancock & David Nathan: *Hancock*

39. Stan Tracey, interviewed by Richard Fawkes

40. Leslie Melville, on the website *butlins-memories.com*

41. *Watford Observer*, 27 June 2013

42. RAFA magazine *Air Mail*, October 1948

43. *Watford Observer*, 16 March 2009

44. Elsa Page/Crawshaw, interviewed in the *Torquay Herald Express*, 8 March 1995

45. Review in *The Stage*, 13 September 1962

46. Dilys Powell: 'A recorded dialogue', *Sunday Times*, 14 & 21 January 1962

IMAGE CREDITS

. . . .

p61   Peter with Dudley Jones: "In Town Tonight". © IWM

p61   "It's the Tops". © IWM

p64   Peter with Jimmy Patton et al in Burma (Paul & Barry Elliott/Patton)

p66   Gang Show no.10 at Koggala. (*My Weekly*)

p71   *The Stage*, 28 June 1945.

p71   Listing from the Isle Of Wight. (Isle of Wight County Press)

p73   Gang Show no.9 (ii) at West Raynham. (Paul Crowe & Susan Waring)

p86   Gang Show no.10 (ii) in Bückeburg. (Babs Adams/Moorley's)

p88   Gang Show no.10 (ii) in Blankenese. (Peter Sellers/The Lynne Unger Children's Trust: courtesy of BFI National Archive)

p92   Peter with his corporal's stripes, 1946. (Peter Sellers/The Lynne Unger Children's Trust: courtesy of BFI National Archive)

p101 Ralph Reader, Cardew Robinson, Dudley Jones, Peter, David Lodge, 1962. (Shutterstock)

p105 Spoof advertisement in the *Calcutta Statesman*? (British Library)

p128 Peter and a pony cart in India. (Peter Sellers/The Lynne Unger Children's Trust: courtesy of BFI National Archive)

. . . .

ACKNOWLEDGEMENTS

Mark J Cousins, for setting me on the path to this project, and mentoring along the way

Tom Quinn, for his invaluable advice and guidance

Richard B Fawkes, for kindly granting me access to his notes and other material collected for the book *Fighting for A Laugh*

Matthew Lee, Helen Upcraft, David Tibbs @ IWM London

Peter Devitt @ RAF Museum, Hendon

Victoria Bennett, Espen Bale @ BFI Special Collections

Neil Raj @ The British Library

Gary Johnson @ Library of Congress, Washington, DC

Alyssa Devine, representing the Lynne Unger Children's Trust, for arranging permission to reproduce photographs from the Peter Sellers Archive

Martin Gibbons & the late Tristan Brittain-Dissont @ The Tony Hancock Appreciation Society

Mrs Soo Chapman (on behalf of The Malcolm Chapman collection)

Mike Hoffman & the late Gordon Blackburn @ The London Gang Show Fellowship

Sue Donnelly @ London School of Economics

Laura Gardiner @ Rotherham Archives

Hugh Comerford, Catherine Gerbrands @ *The Stage*

Alan Marriott @ The Isle of Wight County Press

Barry Sullivan @ DC Thomson Archive

Sharon Hardwick @ St Clement Danes Church

Trevor Hayes @ Abbots Langley RAFA

Pia Walker @ Box & Fiddle Magazine

. . . .

Information, help and contributions came from: Geoff Boudreau, Paul Crowe, Paul Elliott, Graeme Fraser, Zen Grisdale, Nick Messinger, Glen Michael (Cecil Buckland), Tony Mulholland, Ed Sikov, Eddie Whitney

Lastly, a huge thank you to my father, Graham Brownsword, and my friends, Katharine & Martin Kingsbury, for their generous support and encouragement whenever it was needed.

In front of a *tonga* cart, somewhere in India, 1944?
(Fresh off the boat from England, 'by the whiteness of his knees'–
a reliable way of telling how long a serviceman had been in the tropics.)